The High Price of Everything

The High Price of Everything

Stories by Kathleen Coskran

Minnesota Voices Project Number 33

NEW RIVERS PRESS 1988

Copyright © 1988 by Kathleen Coskran
Library of Congress Catalog Card Number: 88-60055
ISBN 0-89823-102-7
All rights reserved
Typesetting: Peregrine Publications
Author and title page photo by Charles Coskran

"Graven Images" first appeared in *The Great River Review*. Our thanks to the editors for permission to reprint here. Photo on title page is of a Makonde sculpture.

The High Price of Everything has been published with the aid of grants from the Jerome Foundation, the First Bank System Foundation, the United Arts Council (with funds provided in part by the McKnight Foundation), and the National Endowment for the Arts (with funds provided by the Congress of the United States).

The author also wishes to thank her editor, Ian Leask, for his careful attention to her work and for his encouragement.

New Rivers Press books are distributed by

The Talman Company
150 - 5th Avenue
New York, NY 10011

The High Price of Everything has been manufactured in the United States of America for New Rivers Press, Inc. (C. W. Truesdale, editor/publisher), 420 N. 5th St., Suite 910, Minneapolis, MN 55401 in a first edition of 1,500 copies. Second printing January 1990, 750 copies.

FOR CHUCK

CONTENTS

IT'S AN ODD COLLECTION of stories, three set in East Africa, five in Georgia. They wouldn't arrange themselves in any coherent pattern until I put them in the order in which they were written. This arrangement revealed my journey as a writer to me. The earlier stories have autobiographical chunks; the later ones come more directly from my imagination. When I look at them together, I see myself moving from worlds I've seen to worlds I imagine.

I was in a village called Lalibela once, high in the Simien Mountains of Ethiopia. Lalibela is a famous holy place; within the town there are ten monolithic churches carved out of the living rock that date to the fourteenth century. I heard of another church beyond the village and walked all one day to find it. I was alone. I crossed high ridges between craters that looked like the surface of the moon; I went through shadowy forests. I passed few people, but those I did pass kept me on the right path. At one point the trail led up the side of an *amba*, or plateau. I switched back and forth on the path for an hour until my head slowly rose above the surface of the *amba* and a broad, flat, sunny field stretched before me at eye level. I felt like Jack climbing off the bean stock into a new world.

I think of that journey when I'm searching for the story in the words I've written. The road is long and hard and I have only a vague sense of where I'm going. I get some help from my friends to keep me on track, but I have to go alone and I never know what I will find or exactly what I am looking for. When I think I'm at the end and my head emerges into the sunlight, I discover a new path. The way is easier then, but the journey's not over until I find a holy place carved out of rock and a priest to let me in.

I crossed that meadow and climbed again to reach the church embedded in rock. A gaunt priest in white robes laid out the treasures of the church: a leather drum, a heavy silver cross for me to kiss, and a large picture of Jesus sitting in a sunny field, surrounded by children. The writing under the picture was in English: " 'Suffer the little children to come unto me'. . . Printed in Oklahoma City, U.S.A." You never know what you're going to find when you get to the end.

Kathleen Coskran
January 24, 1988

The High Price of Everything

MAMA RAPPED ME on the side of the head with her knuckles, then stepped around the highway James and I had chiseled out of the red Georgia clay. "Get on in the house. Both of you," she said and began pulling jeans and stiff towels off the clothesline. Her pony tail swished along the nape of her neck as she thunked the clothespins into the plastic bucket.

I grabbed the yellow cars and trucks we'd cut out of Cheerios boxes and pulled James up by the shoulder of his T-shirt. He took the biggest truck out of my hand and flattened it against his stomach, then slipped it in his pocket. I smashed mine the same way and jammed it in the waistband of my shorts, against my backbone where she wouldn't notice. "What you want us to do, Mama?" I asked.

She glared over the clothesline. Her eyes were as blue and sharp as ever but her face had gone white behind red splotches and her chin trembled slightly when she started to talk. "I want you out of that dirt, Liza. Look at the streaks on that clean blouse," she said.

"These ain't good clothes," I said. "I can hardly wear this old shirt, it's so small." I stuck out my stomach to show her how the blouse split above my shorts.

"They're the clothes you've got, girl. Some example you set for your brother."

She walked past me with her head bent over the towels she carried, to keep the sun out of her eyes, and went in the house, slamming the door behind her. "Pick up those clothespins and get in here," she shouted through the screen.

She probably had a migraine. Those headaches put her to bed shivering on the hottest day in July. I nodded at James and we hurried in the house.

I started right off washing my stained shirt at the kitchen sink, being careful not to splash the dirty water anywhere and got to thinking about school and my clothes. By now Mama was sitting at the table with a mixing bowl in her lap, mixing batter for a cake. "Mama, school starts a week from Tuesday," I said, watching her. I could see the big muscle in her right arm as she beat in the milk and eggs. "What am I going to wear?"

She hit the spoon on the side of the bowl, then stared at me like I was telling a fib.

"I expect you'll wear what you wore last year."

"Those old clothes are too small," I mumbled without looking at her. I squeezed the soap out of my shirt until my arms ached from the effort, then ran clean water in the sink. I heard her beat the batter a couple more strokes, then stop.

"Liza, we bought you three dresses last year — paid good money — and Aunt Caroline brought over that plaid jumper of Sarah Ann's. I don't want to hear no more about it."

"Yes'm."

She bent to the cake batter again, counting the strokes under her breath. I scrubbed my shirt in time with her counting — two hundred one, two hundred two, two hundred three. At the count of five hundred, she stopped beating and scraped the sides of the bowl with the spoon.

"You know we can't afford something new for you every time the styles change, every time Lynda Sue flops in here with the latest this or that," she said, setting the bowl on the table. She wiped the sweat off her forehead with the back of her hand, then pressed two fingers hard against her temple. Her lips spread into a thin, tight line.

*

THE shrill drumming of the cicadas outside and the steady rattling of the attic fan in the hall filled our room that night. I lay on my back and pushed my hair behind my ears so I could pick up their voices from the other bedroom. It was easy to hear Daddy — he had the voice of a hog caller — but he spoke in such short sentences that I couldn't always tell what his meaning was.

"I know she needs clothes. I need clothes. You need clothes. Look at you. Look at us. She can't have everything she thinks she needs."

I had to prop up on my elbows to hear Mama.

". . . woman now . . . needs something nice."

I couldn't catch it all. James was sleeping like a hound dog, spread across his pillow with his thumb falling out of his mouth, so I got up quietly and stood in the shadow of the door.

"How do you expect to pay for it?"

"We don't need that much. If you'd let me take out a charge account, it wouldn't be so hard."

"Damn it, Sylvia. No."

He must have sat up — it sounded like his words dropped from the ceiling. "You know what I think about store credit. That's what's killing people around here. We pay for what we get."

"Quiet. You'll wake the children." Mama spoke like she was talking to me, sharp and fast. "Wendall, they've got to have clothes. I can't stand to see what they're wearing."

"What I see is that I'm working two jobs and my wife's not satisfied."

"It's not your fault. I'm the one who got laid off. Jewel Foods will be calling me back any day now. You'll see."

They were quiet and then I heard Mama's voice come back like a fiddle playing, low and sweet. "Wendall, we could open just one tiny charge account — and pay it off the minute I'm called back to work. We won't use my wages for anything else, until it's paid off."

"Did you hear me? We aren't opening no accounts. It's a trap. I won't be trapped."

"I heard you, Wendall." The fiddle left Mama's voice and she purred the way an old cat does when it rubs up your leg. "Just give me fifteen dollars out of this check and fifteen out of the next. I promise you I won't ask for no more."

The bed creaked and I heard his bare feet slap the floor. I stepped back into my room and caught sight of myself in that little mirror

3

from Walgreen's. I turned sideways and pulled my nightgown tight at the waist. Not much shape to me that I could see, but it was pretty dark. I slid under the covers before anybody saw me.

*

I WAS in bed the next morning, when I heard Mama on the phone to Grandma. "Mama M., can you mind James for a day? Liza and I have to go to Atlanta."

I got up quickly and went out to the kitchen to get my cereal so I could hear what she was saying.

"Yes, ma'am. You know he's no trouble. We'll bring his cars and blanket for a nap." Mama waved her finger at me and smiled like she had a secret.

Mama didn't trust Grandma — she thought she spent too much time drinking iced tea and waddling around her yard watering plants — so she started listing her warnings: don't let him go outside alone; see that he washes before he eats; bring him inside if there are bees or wasps out. I once saw Mama step between six squealing piglets and an angry sow without looking scared at all, but she made herself sick thinking about everything that could happen to us, especially James. In a way, James' being so sickly and all and such a difficult birth had made things a lot easier for me. Still, every time I left the house, even to go to school, Mama would say, "I'll kill you if something happens to you." She'd say it like she was telling a joke, but I knew she meant it — her brother TJ drowned in a swimming hole when he was eleven and Mama was eight. Daddy told me about TJ once when we were having a talk about how I ought to be patient and respect Mama more.

*

WE went to Atlanta the next week. Daddy dropped us on the square in Clintock and, as Mama went into Bolton's to get the bus tickets, he took my arm and whispered in my ear, "You see that your mother takes it easy, that she gets a coke and something to eat. You hear?"

"Yes, sir."

"You know what'll happen if she gets tired out and don't eat?"

4

"Yes, sir, she'll get a migraine and throw up all over everything."

He looked at me like he was mad but just then Mama came back to the truck. "Wendall, you call your mother at lunch time and see if she needs anything for James. And be back here at six. You know I can't stand waiting."

Irene Campbell worked the front register at Bolton's Drug Store, to attract customers, people said, because she was so pretty. My best friend, Lynda Sue Lancaster, claimed that Irene bleached her hair, wore false fingernails, and smeared on a pound of make-up every day, but that was okay by me. I wanted to know how she got the fingernails to stay on and if her eyelashes were fake, but I never got up the nerve to ask. Irene didn't like children.

"One full, one half-fare for Atlanta," Mama said and pushed a ten dollar bill across the counter.

"Liza's going with you, ain't she? She pay full fare now," Irene said.

"Of course Liza's going. You see anybody else standing here?"

Mama set her purse on the counter and wrapped both arms around the old bag and leaned toward Irene. "But she's just a child. She pay half-fare, like always."

"How old are you, Liza?" Irene asked, looking over Mama's shoulder at me.

I started to tell her but saw a funny look in Mama's eyes and look-ed back at the schedule posted on the wall.

"You must be 'bout 12 now. Is that right?"

I nodded without taking my eyes off the schedule.

"Thought so."

Irene punched the keys on the ticket board with her nails held aloft so they didn't get snagged, then slid two tickets across the counter. "That'll be two full fares to Atlanta for eight dollars, Sylvia," she said.

"Now, look here, Irene, you can't go changing the rules on us. I always pay half-fare for Liza. You got no right to charge me full price."

"The rules are the same, Sylvia. It's your girl who's changed. She's 12 and got to pay accordingly."

Irene wet the pad of her little finger on her tongue, then slowly pulled the damp finger across the skin under her left eye, catching dots of mascara. "Eight dollars, please," she said.

"We'll see about that."

Mama rose up on her toes like a copperhead swaying over some poor, small animal. Irene licked her finger again and went at the other eye, but I backed away and stood by the door. Mama swished past me and I followed her out.

"What a stupid girl. Did you see the fingernails on her?"

Mama paced back and forth in the shade at the corner of the store, her purse swinging ahead of her, then banging on her hip bone. "Irene Campbell is a stuck-up hussy, everybody says so. She's got a baby girl but no husband I can see."

I was real still — didn't say anything, didn't move.

After a minute Mama started yelling at me. "Damn it, Liza, I don't have an extra two dollars for your ticket. This money's for your shoes and a dress for the first day and we've got to get James something decent." She walked to the end of the block and back again. "You're too big, that's what, just too damn big."

"I don't have to go this year. I don't care." I folded my arms and looked away. It would be better if I didn't go. "I'll just wait here until you get back."

"Oh, you can't do that. Your daddy's gone."

"Yes, ma'am, I can. I'll wait right here until six when you get back and he picks us both up."

"You don't have anything to eat."

"Neither do you."

I didn't look at her and I don't think she looked at me. I noticed that when I moved my feet in my old shoes, I could see the different outline of each toe. I peeked at Mama and she was staring at the sky. So we stood there for quite a spell, right on the square at the corner of Main and Green.

"Oh, Liza," She sounded better. "Oh, Liza, you know I can't shop without you, especially for shoes."

"I don't have to have shoes."

"Stay here, girl, and don't leave this spot." Mama put her purse over her arm, straightened her waistband, smoothed her collar, and went back in the drug store.

When she came out, she smiled but not like she meant it.

"Well, I bought them: two front row seats for Atlanta."

She smiled again with her whole face and touched my hair. "We may as well enjoy them," she said.

All the air squeezed out of me like I'd been holding my breath and I started to laugh. There was something else wonderful in the air. I jumped up and took a couple of steps, like I was walking in my sleep. "Mama, do you smell that?"

Mama laughed. "You ought to be in pictures, Liza, the way you carry on. It's just Miz Ellis in the Cherokee Cafe, got her cinnamon rolls done."

I knew the smell was those rolls and remembered that once, for no reason at all, Mama had gone in that restaurant like she did it all the time and bought one of those rolls to split with me. It seemed that this day was just as special and as out of the ordinary as that other day. "Mama," I said, "let's split us a roll. You know how you love them. Nobody'll know."

I'd grabbed her hand and she slapped me, pushing my arm away. "Girl, you grabbed my arthritic finger." She cradled the weak finger in her other hand. "Think, Liza. Don't you know why we can't buy a cinnamon roll, today of all days?"

"We did once," I said, but I don't think she heard me.

She crossed the street to sit in the shade of the bandstand until the bus came and I followed her. I wanted to go shopping and I wanted new clothes so I watched her closely to know how to act.

*

WHEN we got to Atlanta, we followed our usual routine. First we checked out the bargain basements to price clothes, underwear, and school supplies. Mama refused to buy anything before twelve o'clock on principle, because it was important to research thoroughly before you put down money.

It was after noon when we sat down in the children's shoe department. I wondered what she was thinking; my feet were way too big for those kiddie shoes.

"Mama, we can't sit here. We can't get my size in this department any more," I whispered.

"Quiet, we've got work to do. Nobody's using these chairs."

"But, Mama . . ."

She wasn't listening so I tried to forget about it. She handed me a couple sheets of paper that she had been making notes on.

"Time to discuss our strategy," she announced.

I loved this part. Mama talked very fast when she planned, mimicking salesgirls she had sloughed off. " 'What can I help you girls with today?' As if I'm a girl at thirty-plus," she said. "They wear false smiles and don't do a real day's work and they just hang on you, like they know your business and what you should have. Make it a point, Liza, never to buy anything one of those girls has told you is cute."

I thought the salesgirls with their shiny shoes and red lips were beautiful. I liked to look at their smooth hands and sharp, colored nails. The way they could hold a pen and know just how to fill out a sales slip was something, and they all had a piece of plastic pinned on their soft blouses with their names − Lily or Claire or Mary Ann. I never saw a Liza, but once a woman, an older woman, wore a tag that said LISA. I wondered if Mama had spelled my name wrong.

"May I help you, girls?"

A tall man, blond and smooth-shaven, bent over Mama, his hands stuck deep in his pockets like Daddy's when he's looking over the fence at something gone wrong with the pigs. His eyes and suit were the same color of brown. I couldn't stop staring at him, but Mama took her time noticing him.

She finally looked up. "No, thank you. We're being helped by somebody else."

He walked away.

"Mama, that's a lie."

"No, Liza, it's not," she said, smiling like she was teaching me something. "We are being taken care of by somebody else − ourselves. If he thinks I meant something different by those words, I can't help it, but I did not lie to that boy."

She turned back to her chart of best buys.

"Okay, let's see − panties, socks, and T-shirts. Where are the best deals? Check your sheets, Liza."

"Panties are four for $5.50 at Walgreen's, three for $4.50 at Rich's, and two for $3.25 in Davison's basement," I read.

"Why don't they package everything the same? Let me think." Mama was quick with math.

"The dime store's are cheaper but I wasn't going to buy four. You could get along with three or even two, couldn't you?"

"Are you interested in shoes, ma'am?"

That man was back, bending over Mama again.

She continued to write, transferring information from her notes to her chart. I stared at him so he'd know we were listening, and maybe he'd be patient until Mama was ready. He stared back at me with large, moist eyes and I held my breath. Then he looked at Mama and then back at me, and the dark part in his eyes floated.

"You can't loiter, ma'am, if you're not interested in shoes." He was talking to the top of Mama's head. "I'll have to call the manager," he said. He looked at me, making my stomach go weak, and then he hurried away through a door marked Store Personnel Only.

As soon as he left, Mama stood up.

"Let's get going — we're done here."

She folded the papers, put them in her purse and walked swiftly towards the main aisle. I ran after her.

She stopped at a pay phone. "I reckon it wouldn't hurt to call and see how James is doing," she said.

"Mama, he's fine. It costs money to call all the way home."

She opened her purse to look for change. "Not so much," she said. "What are you going to do if he's not all right?"

Sometimes she scared me with all her worry about James. She made me feel all tight inside and I was just getting over the weak feeling from the man in the shoe department. Mama couldn't let anything be.

I heard the money slide down the length of the phone and ring the bell.

"I can't do anything, but I want to know," she said.

After the call she smiled at me like I was company and put her arm around my shoulders. "You're my big girl now. You know that, Sugar?"

She squeezed me to her breast and I put my arm around her waist. "It's such fun shopping with my grown-up daughter," she said.

"You feel all right, Mama? No migraines?" I asked. She looked so happy, I was glad she'd called about James.

"I feel great, Liza. Your daddy's got you worrying about me too much. Just relax and enjoy the shopping."

I said I'd try, and I did, because I certainly did not want to be a worry wart like her.

We were on the mezzanine in Rich's, just passing through, when we saw this blue dress on a mannequin in the junior high department. Mama noticed it first and said it was the color of my eyes. She lifted the skirt to show me the deep hem and fine material, a sure sign of quality. I thought the model looked a little like me with skinny arms and dishwater blond hair.

"Oh, it's so pretty, Mama." I stood next to the mannequin and pulled the big skirt over my dress. "How do I look?"

"It's certainly your color, Liza. It is beautiful."

We stood in front of the dress for a long time, the way we stand and look at the Christmas tree after it has all the lights and tinsel on. Mama pointed out the lines of the dress, the fine stitching, the stylish details. We both held the cloth to our cheeks. Then I saw a salesgirl leave her cash register to walk towards us. I held my breath and looked at Mama. She dropped the hem of the dress. "Let's go, Liza. It's a pretty price, I'm sure."

"Mama." I hurried to catch up. "Mama, it wouldn't hurt to try it on, would it? I know we can't buy it." I grabbed her arm — I wanted just to see what I could look like. "I probably don't even need it, but it would be part of our research."

"It's a waste of our time."

She shook off my hand without slowing up a bit. "It's a waste of time," she said softly, "and it might hurt."

That dress had a power over me — I couldn't stop thinking how I would look walking into school in that blue dress. Lynda Sue would just die when she saw me. And Henry Ledbetter, well, he would probably look at me the way Daddy looked at Mama after she washed her hair. I saw myself standing in the bathroom at home, looking in the mirror, with some of Mama's blue eye shadow on and my hair done up in a French twist. I could be as pretty as her. I knew it was no use, but I begged her again, like a little kid, "Mama, please. I just want to see how I'd look in something so pretty."

"Liza, I told you no. We got things to do."

She grabbed my hand and walked faster. She pulled me through the store, out on the street and into the next store before I could think what to say. I hadn't felt her hold me so hard and tight in a long time. My hand was dripping wet when she let go. So was my face — I had been crying about that fool dress. I wiped my eyes with my dry hand. It was hot and I was hungry. I thought of Daddy and knew that we better eat because Mama needed food even more than me or she would get one of those headaches and Daddy would kill me. But I was afraid to say anything and still mad about the dress. It wouldn't have hurt a thing to try it on, so I didn't mention lunch. She never had time to eat anyway, not shopping, not when we'd have to pay those high prices for everything and the food was barely fit to eat. So I kept quiet; I wouldn't see Daddy for hours and Mama was with me now, changed like Snow White's step-mother — her hair all strung-out ringlets and her face hard and sweaty.

By four o'clock Rich's was crowded with people, but we were almost done. I leaned on a glass counter, admiring the scarves displayed below, while she paid for the navy skirt that would go with everything.

I watched her count out the money and we both smiled when there was more than a dollar left over. "Would you like to open a charge account? You can fill out a form today," the saleswoman said. Her name tag said FAY W.

Mama hesitated, then shook her head. "No, thank you."

Fay W. was a weasel-faced woman with slicked back, grey hair, sprayed hard and pulled into a bun. Her hair was perfect — no wisps escaped to curl around her ears. She wore thick rouge and her glasses hung around her neck. She put the glasses on and handed Mama a charge account application. "Well, at least look at it. It is so convenient — everybody's getting them — and I get a bonus for every good customer I sign up."

Mama looked at the paper, then handed it back, shaking her head, "No, I can't do it now."

Fay W. smiled without showing her teeth. "You people are mak-ing a big mistake. You've got to keep up with the new way of doing business," she said.

"We're not ignorant," Mama said and slapped her purse on the counter. "I know all about credit. I just don't want it. It's a trap." She put out her hand for the package.

Fay W. looked at me as she handed Mama the bag. "Tell your girl to keep her dirty hands off the display case. It leaves prints."

I jammed my hands in my pockets and looked at Mama.

"Her hands aren't dirty," Mama said, and then I heard somebody laughing just behind me and saying, "I bet they are dirty — just like her dress."

I looked out of the side of my eye to see two high school girls. They had the same hair and skirts, just like a picture in *Seventeen* magazine.

The taller girl whispered, "Poor skinny thing. The dress is just stained and faded." Then they were laughing about something.

I looked around to see who they were talking about. There was nobody close but me and Mama and Fay W. I looked at my hands. They were clean, pink, and no dirt in the creases. Maybe they weren't even talking about me. My dress was clean — it was my favorite. When it was new it was the color of soft, new pine needles in May and if you opened the folds at the waist that fresh, green color was still there.

Mama handed me the package. "Let's go, Liza." Her voice was so low that I had to look up to hear her. She bent over me as we walked out. "Those were silly girls and that was one dumb saleswoman. Don't forget that — they were stupid."

"Am I really skinny, Mama?"

She stopped on the street, looked at me carefully and shook her head. "You're just fine, Liza, just fine. You'll be a pretty woman," she said. "Don't think about those ugly girls." Mama's face was pale and splotched and her chin shook, but she made me feel better and not so much like crying.

We got to the bus station twenty minutes early. I found seats together for us away from other people. As soon as we sat down, Mama rested her head on her knuckles and rubbed her forehead.

"Are you feeling all right, Mama?"

"I'm fine," she said. "Just tired."

"You have a headache."

I could tell by her eyes and the way she held her head. "Don't you want me to get you a coke?" I asked.

She carefully shook her head and didn't want to talk to me.

"Shall I call about James — see if he's still okay?"

"No . . . no. Just go do something, look around, get some exercise. But be back here in time to help me get all this stuff on the bus." She raised her head. "Don't talk to anybody."

"Can I wear my new shoes?"

She nodded.

I took off those old things that curled my toes up and put on the clean, white Keds we had bought. They looked nice. I wiggled my toes inside to feel all the room and got up to try them out. First I walked around the edge of the waiting room, stopped before all the vending machines, read the prices of the candy bars and crackers. In one machine there was an apple for twenty cents. Funny to think of somebody buying an apple out of a machine. Then I had to go to the bathroom and got there just in time to see this fat woman put a dime in the cologne machine and spray herself. She held the button with one finger, raised her neck to the spray and then quickly twirled around spreading her arms like crow's wings to get the cologne all over her. Some of it landed on me as I walked past her to the stall.

Mama was standing, gathering the packages when I got back. "Thought I was going to have to do this myself," she said.

I took the bags from her and we got in the line outside the terminal door, me first.

"Oh, Liza," Mama put her hand on my shoulder. "I can't take these diesel fumes. And somebody's got on cheap perfume. Goes straight to my head."

I leaned over the packages I was holding to sniff my arms and they smelled just like the fat woman in the bathroom. I tried to move the bags from side to side, rubbing them along my skin to get the scent off.

I found two empty seats as near the front of the bus as possible. I knew she couldn't stand the fish-tail sway of the back of the bus so late in the day and with no lunch. "You sit by the window, Mama," I said.

She took the inside seat and I began arranging the packages overhead, but she stopped me. "We've got plenty of room. Put all those bags here, on the floor, by our feet. We might want to get something."

"You have a migraine, don't you?"

I knew she did and wondered how we'd ever make it home and what Daddy would do to me when we got there. It was a fifty-mile ride on a full bus.

We hadn't been going fifteen minutes when Mama touched me on the arm. "I'm going to need a bag, Liza. Sorry." Her skin was flat white like the Walgreen sack. She leaned into the window so the whole side of her face touched the cool glass.

"Do you want me to open the window first?" I said.

"No, Honey, just get a bag."

I pulled socks and underwear out of a bag, crammed them into a larger sack, and handed the empty one to Mama.

She put the bag to her mouth as if she were going to blow it up, then she started to cough and heave, slowly at first, and then faster. She reminded me of a cat with a hairball, straining to get it out. I tried to turn sideways in my seat and face her and kind of spread over her because other people were looking.

When she was done, I gave her a tissue and took the bag, rolled the top down tightly, and slipped it under my seat. We were 40 miles from home. Mama closed her eyes and let her head lay back on the seat.

She needed two more bags and both times she whispered, "Oh, Liza, I'm so sorry."

"It's okay," I said and I meant it because I knew what to do and maybe she could get to feeling better before we got home.

I had to stuff everything into one bag that was spilling over so I held that one on my lap and put the three rolled-up packages in a row under my seat. When we were nearly home, she put her hand on my leg and I put my hand on hers to let her know everything was all right and then I lay back to rest too. As soon as I closed my eyes, I saw myself wearing the blue dress, twirling around and around in front of that little mirror at home, straining to see how I looked. I opened my eyes and looked at Mama. She had pulled the tight rubber band off her pony tail and her yellow hair spread across her shoulder like corn silk. She leaned against the window with her lips slightly parted, breathing through her mouth. Her shallow breaths smelled sweet and stale and there were dark circles under her eyes where her mascara had smeared. Depending on the way things were when we got home, I decided to ask if I could try some of that mascara and the baby blue eye shadow.

An African River

"THE ANUAK sleep in the ashes of their cooking fires," I read from *National Geographic*, loosening my frayed seat belt and nudging Walker. He was staring across the aisle of the plane, watching a man with warrior scars on his forehead page the *Herald Tribune*.

"It's mosquito prevention," I said. "Isn't that fascinating?"

"Are you telling me we have reservations in a bed of ashes?" He unwrapped the candy the stewardess had given him, put it in his mouth and handed me the wrapper. "How remote is this place? Is there a train station?"

I laughed. "I don't think so," I said. "There goes your entree into sophisticated conversation. You'll have to learn another phrase."

Walker had an M.B.A. from Harvard and was a visiting in-structor at Haile Selassie University in Addis Ababa, but he spoke only four words of Amharic: "Where is the train station?" Whenever we were lost, confused, or he was bored, he would ask the nearest Ethiopian for directions to the train station. He said speaking the language made him feel a part of things, important for a black man.

"I don't need another phrase. We have no business going to a place without trains."

The man across the aisle dumped a box of rifle shells on the newspaper spread over his lap, then he touched each shell to his tongue, tamped it with his thumb, and twisted it through a loop on the wide leather belt draped across his chest.

"Jesus," Walker said. "I wonder where he's getting off."

I handed him my camera. "Here. It's all set," I said. "Take his picture."

"Are you crazy?" Walker whispered. "What if he's Muslim and believes that his soul gets trapped in the little black box? I don't want him mad at us."

"I don't see a gun," I said.

"Look on the floor."

The man's black boots rested on the barrel of a carbine.

"Ask him if he knows where the train station is."

Walker laughed and shook his head. "You always get it backwards, Margaret. This is not a joking dude."

The man across the aisle held the gun belt over the empty seat next to the window and shook it, then hunched forward and strapped it around his waist. He picked up the carbine and propped it between his knees, the barrel pointing at his shoulder. He pulled a cigarette out of his pocket and leaned across the aisle to Walker. "Matches?" he said.

Walker nodded and gave him a disposable lighter. "Keep it."

The man grinned with wide, flat teeth and grabbed Walker's hand with both of his in a gesture of gratitude. "May God know you," he said in Amharic.

"Nice guy," Walker said when the man released him. He let his eyes roll back in his head and wiped his forehead with his handkerchief. "Part of the adventure?"

"Just the beginning," I said. "We're going to see real Africa this time."

"Have I mentioned that I'm on this pleasure cruise under protest?"

"Several times. And I appreciate your coming."

He waved me off. "My father should be here, not me," he said, staring past me, out the window. "Look at that shit out there."

The plane was in a descent, dropping into barren land. There were no forests, no cultivated fields, few huts. The only sign of life was a narrow ribbon of green on either side of a river that curved through flat, colorless country.

"This is what he wanted, you know. I've been thinking this whole year that he should be here, not me, and let them call him foreigner and let him see what a stinking mess everything is." He wiped his face with his handkerchief and leaned across me. "Why are we dropping? I don't see a landing field."

"I'm sure there's a strip somewhere. It's a scheduled stop — Gebele — where the Anuak live." I showed him the magazine picture. "We'll get off and look around."

He shook his head and nodded in the direction of the man with the carbine. "Not me. The place isn't big enough for both of us."

The man had folded his newspaper and jammed it in his trousers next to his backbone, adjusting the gun belt as he did so. The carbine slipped and the barrel fell across the aisle, towards us. Walker pushed it back with one finger and the man smiled at him again.

"We could think of this whole trip as a carnival ride. Stay on for the full circuit and be back in Addis by sundown," he said.

I ignored him as I had been ignoring his nervous protestations about the trip for a month because I knew if I listened to him we wouldn't go. We had been married less than a year and my stomach stirred every time I looked at him. He had skin the color of burnt sugar and a chiseled face that revealed every detail of the skeletal structure of his head. His body was hard, the skin stretched over bone and muscle until he smiled and it made me weak to look at him. I realize now how young I was, how frivolous, always looking for new experiences to amuse Walker so he would turn his head and grin in his conspiratorial way. I watched him all the time.

The plane touched down. Two children and an old man with goats hurried just beyond the sweep of the wing. Our shadow washed over them and the smallest boy scooped up a kid and disappeared in a clutch of huts under the trees near the river. The man with the carbine stood up, adjusted his overcoat, held the gun in his left hand and offered his right to Walker. "Good morning, ferengie."

Walker looked startled, then stuck out his hand. "Good bye, Ethiopian," he said.

A woman with a baby on her hip stopped in the aisle to stare at us. She pointed and said, "Ferengie," to her child.

Walker gripped the sagging armrest. "I hate being called foreigner. It's a conspiracy to torment me, Margaret."

I couldn't understand why it upset him so. Ethiopians shouted ferengie at all foreigners. "It's what we are, Walker, both of us, ferengies."

"Yeah."

"Well?"

"You act like this country is the latest exhibit at Disneyland. It's not. It's real." He flexed his fingers and stared at the backs of his hands. "My father said I'd be home if I ever got to Africa. You should have heard him, preaching like Moses."

"I did hear him." His father had called me a white witch.

"So, he was wrong."

The plane was nearly empty. "Let's get off, stretch our legs. It'll do you good," I said.

He shook his head. "I can't. You go ahead." He closed his eyes. "I'm too hot to move."

"Okay," I said and stepped over him to the aisle. "I'll be right back."

*

ON the runway I hesitated midway between the edge of the strip and the plane, squinting into the sun. It was hot and there wasn't much to see: a shack for a terminal, with a faded sign that said Gebele Airport in English and Amharic. An impromptu market with gourds, cloth and empty coke bottles flanked the little building. A boy about six poked a stick through a covered basket, tormenting the chicken inside, while the owner gossiped with the woman next to her.

I got out my camera and squatted in the sand to focus on the boy. When I looked up, I locked eyes with a woman selling empty tins. She gasped and covered her mouth. From behind me, a second woman appeared, pushed me aside, snatched the boy away from the chicken, threw him over her shoulder, and ran off, shrieking. The other women stared at me, frozen and solemn, as if I were a ghost. I rose slowly and brushed the dust from my skirt. I slipped my camera in my bag and looked around for Walker. The plane was motionless on the landing strip; I couldn't see his face at any of the small black windows.

"I'm sure they've seen a white woman before," I whispered to myself.

"Yes, you very white, Madam." She startled me, a girl in a school uniform smiling pleasantly, speaking English. She could have been one of my students. She took my elbow in her small hand and tried to steer me towards a path. "You come with me."

She was slight and lovely with the delicate features characteristic of highland women. I touched her shoulder and shook my head. "I can't. My plane is leaving in a few minutes."

"I know," the girl enunciated carefully. "It is no problem. Come."

There was no movement near the plane and I could hear the pilot and stewardess laughing inside the terminal. "Okay," I said, "just for a minute." I advanced my film and checked the light reading. Walker would be sorry he stayed on the plane.

We followed a path that curved away from the airstrip and over a rise in the land. I turned around once and the plane was out of sight. We quickly reached a wide clearing. Clay pots, clothing, spear heads, onions were spread on bamboo mats in uneven rows. Goats and camels were staked at the far end; a blacksmith pounded iron under a tree as a small boy worked the bellows. The air was heavy with the odor of spices and of the oils and butters women spread on their skin and hair.

"You wanted me to see this?"

The girl nodded. "Come."

As we entered the market, a wave of silence spread before us. I had heard of this phenomenon, a whole market focusing on one ferengie, but it had never happened to me. The people were tall and quite black and wore few clothes. An enormous man clad only in ostrich shell beads at his waist and playing a finger piano bent in front of me so his great head was inches from my face. The student said something I didn't understand and he straightened up and let us pass. The people abandoned their bartering to fan out as I passed, trampling gourds and potatoes under their feet, following me. Hands brushed my head and face like gnats, bristling the hairs on my arms. A woman with a string of blue beads dangling from her lower lip thrust a newborn baby in my face and said, "Take her; take her," in Amharic. I tried to respond but the girl pulled me on. We crossed the clearing and stood before a chika hut, one of those temporary bars where you could get a local beer or *tej* poured out of a teapot on market day.

"Your husband is here," she said in English.

I laughed. "My husband is sulking on the plane."

The girl pushed me through the open door.

The abrupt change from light to dark blinded me momentarily. "I can't see anything," I said.

The people crowded around the doorway and window, darkening the tiny room further. The lumpy mud and straw walls took on human form.

"You have made a mistake," I said in the voice I use with my problem students. I was damp with a cold sweat and didn't know what game we were playing. The reference to a husband was unnerving. "I can't stay," I said.

They stared past me to the corner of the room. A man wrapped in a shamma and wearing a large brimmed hat and dark glasses sat, bent over, on a low stool in the deepest shadow of the bar, facing the mud wall. A woman holding a dented teapot put her hand to her mouth when she saw me and backed away.

I stood in the center of the little room. The girl began to speak in a rapid, high voice, pointing at the man in the corner but not looking in his direction. He pulled his hat close to his ears and slowly turned to face the beam of light from the doorway. I thought of the lepers outside the church in Addis on holy days and wondered what afflicted this man. The girl's voice became insistent. The man stood up and shuffled across the room. He stretched his hand towards me and the paleness of his palm was like a beacon in the dim room. The girl pushed me forward. He grasped my hands firmly and I knew he was not a cripple.

"Who are you?" I whispered in English. I couldn't see his face under the hat and wondered if he were some sort of ferengie political prisoner.

He led me to the door without speaking. The people backed away and we stepped into the bright light of the market. I thought of running but the crowd held the circle together and the man grasped my hand firmly. I took a slow, deep breath and looked at his face. His skin was so thin that I could see blood moving in his puffy jaw. He wore mirrored glasses that reflected my pale face. He pointed to his dark glasses and then to me and spoke in a thundering Amharic. "Take off your glasses."

"He wants me to remove my glasses?"

"Yes, Madam."

A shadow traveled across the clearing and everybody looked up at a cloud covering the sun, then the people turned back to me with a single movement, waiting. I took off my dark glasses, dropped them in my bag, and stared at the stranger, trying not to blink.

The man removed his glasses and met my gaze with bright pink eyes, the red eyes of people in flash snapshots taken with cheap film. He looked like the white rabbit in *Alice in Wonderland*, a chubby, pale man with pink eyes, dressed in a rumpled suit. A murmur rose from the crowd.

"Your eyes are different, Madam," the girl said.

"Yes." I laughed and wiped my face with a trembling hand. "You thought I was albino like him." The encounter had unnerved me. He was just a man. I shook his hand, smiling with relief. He was really quite short. "I have a plane to catch. Good-bye."

A woman ran towards me, yanked my long hair and dashed back, giggling, holding two blond strands. Two men began to argue and the crowd separated into small groups. Nobody followed me as I walked away. I started to run, skirting vegetables and chickens. I felt the tremor and roar of a plane taking off, then a shadow passed overhead. I stopped and looked up, puzzled. There was only one plane a week in Gebele. Where had this other one come from? I glanced across the market; nobody was watching me any more. I looked up at the plane disappearing in the west and realized that it was my plane. Walker had left me, laughing and smoking, looking out the window.

"Damn him," I shouted and walked faster. He's escaped me, I thought, and is on his way back to Addis.

When I arrived at the landing strip, I was panting, gasping, and furious. The runway was empty. I followed faint tracks in the sandy hard pack to where the plane had been. I looked all around. I couldn't believe that he would leave without me. I gulped the hot air to still my panic and walked the length of the deserted airstrip. The little market was gone. I thought of the Anuak and started to laugh. Maybe somebody will let me sleep in their ashes. I don't have anything else. When I reached the terminal I saw my green and gold airlines bag propped against the whitewashed wall. I should have been relieved to see my stuff but I was enraged. He threw my bag off the plane before he left me. It made the abandonment more deliberate.

I grabbed the bag and stepped inside the dim terminal.

Walker sat rigid on his suitcase, smoking a cigarette, just beyond the doorway.

I shrieked and ran at him but he stood up with his arm out to stop me. "Don't touch me, Margaret. It's hot as hell here."

"Walker, you scared me to death. I thought you'd deserted me."

"Where the hell have you been? I've been yelling at the pilot, making a scene, screaming like an idiot. The asshole wouldn't wait — 'We have firm schedule, sir.' I should have left you, Margaret. I can't believe you did this to me." He threw his cigarette on the dirt floor and stepped on it.

"I'm sorry. I didn't realize..."

"I don't want to hear it." He turned towards me. "I suppose you had some sort of adventure?"

"Well, I was on my way to the train station when this weird little guy . . ."

"Shit, Margaret." He put his arms around me and I dropped my bag.

"You scared me to death," he said in my ear. "Where the hell have you been?" His shirt was limp with sweat. He kissed my hair, then held me at arm's length. "Are you all right?"

"Yes," I said, touching his face. "I'm sorry, Walker. I was so scared when I thought you'd left without me."

"And mad as hell?"

I laughed. "That too." I told him about the albino and the market. The more I talked, the more excited I became. "This is a fabulous place. Wait 'til you see the people — they're tall and handsome like you."

"So now what do we do?"

"We'll just get the plane on Sunday."

He raised his eyebrows and scratched his neck. Then he put his hands on his hips and walked around his suitcase a couple of times, shaking his head. "Great. In other words, make the best of it for the next five days?"

I nodded, trying to conceal my excitement about our unplanned stop.

"It's so damn hot, I can't breathe without sweating." He stuffed his tie in his pocket. "I'm overdressed."

"You usually are. You'll feel better when you can change clothes," I said.

"So, let's get a taxi or gari or something and get to wherever we're going. I need a beer."

"There's nothing on wheels here. We walk — it's part of the adventure."

"Don't be cheerful, Margaret." He grabbed both our bags and stomped past me, through the door, out to the heat and the sun. His lips were pressed thin against his teeth. I knew if I touched his chest I would feel his heart fluttering like a bird's.

A bend in the path and a slight descent led us away from the market, towards the river, and into town. The village was orderly, clean, quiet. The streets looked swept, the huts were arranged in jagged rows, and the few people we saw were tall, healthy, and lacked the curiosity of the people in the market. There were no beggars and nobody ran after us shouting, "Ferengie, ferengie."

"See, Walker," I said, "these people look like you. They have your height and beautiful skin."

He sat down on his suitcase, pulled out his handkerchief and dabbed at the lines of sweat along his hairline and under his nose. "These people are black as a Watusi. They make me look like a different species."

A woman with a baby on her hip and multiple rows of bride beads ringing her neck stood in the sparse shade of an acacia tree, staring at us. I held up my light meter and took a reading.

"You'll make me crazy, playing Margaret Bourke-White among the natives while I'm dissolving in the heat. Where are we staying? Can we get reservations at the Holiday Inn or what?"

I photographed the woman from several angles while she stared contentedly at Walker.

"I'll ask her," I said. Grinning at the young mother, I pantomined sleeping and eating and she handed me her baby. The child grabbed on to my hips with her legs and I felt my blood loop through my body. So this is what it feels like to be a mother, I thought. I touched the baby's smooth face and showed her to Walker.

"Do you want to hold her?"

He stood up and nodded to the mother. She was ebony-skinned, bare-breasted, lovely. Walker spoke slowly. "Where is the train station?" he asked in Amharic.

"She only speaks Anuak," I said.

The woman smiled and pointed to the path ahead of us and then made a jab to the left.

"You just have to know how to talk to them," Walker said and picked up his suitcase.

*

WE found the bar by the noise of the generator that powered the refrigerator. Three Anuak men stood outside the place smoking small clay pipes with bowls carved like heads. An Indian and a white man in a pith helmet sprawled on low stools in front. Through the open doorway — there was no door — we saw a room with a dirt floor, a table with no chairs, and an old Frigidaire leaning in the corner of the room. Like everything else, the building was whitewashed chika. The mud had worn through in places and was beginning to crumble around the base of the walls. A magazine photograph of Haile Selassie hung over the refrigerator.

"Eh, Memsahib, you look hot. Come, sit." The Asian offered me his stool. The white man clenched a cigar in his crack of a mouth and balanced a rifle between his legs. His jaw jutted off-center, as if it had been broken. With marbles for eyes set in an elongated face, he resembled a lizard.

"Can we get a beer here?"

"Yes, Memsahib." The Asian took my money and brought us two sweating bottles of Menelik beer. We sat back to back on Walker's suitcase. I rubbed the cool bottle on my face.

"Say," Walker said to the reptilian man, "where's the action around here?"

The man removed the cigar and yawned, exposing a gold tooth filed to a point. "You Americans?"

"Yeah, Americans," Walker said. "You're British?"

"Kenyan." He pulled a ragged passport out of his pocket and flipped it open to the picture. "See, Republic of Kenya. I am a real African." The man sucked on his teeth and closed the passport.

Walker nodded. "So, what are you, a white hunter?"

"You want to hunt? I'll find you crocodiles, hippos, oryx. If you want to hunt at night, it's cooler, but more expensive."

Walker lit a cigarette. "No, we're not rich. I mean, what's happening here?"

The white hunter looked at me. "You've got a woman already."
Walker nudged me with his elbow.

The Asian grunted. "Nothing happens here."

The beer and the heat made me a little dazed, but I was relieved by Walker's show of interest. "That's why we left Addis, remember? To find a place where nothing happens. It's just a slight change of plans that this is the place."

Walker offered the men cigarettes. They each took two and the Asian brought out more beer. Walker leaned against me on the suitcase and began to hum, to tap his foot and move his shoulders. "You got any music here, records, jazz?"

The hunter snorted and shook his head.

Walker got his third beer from the refrigerator and straddled the suitcase again. "Hey, man," he looked at the Asian. "We've got a little problem. My wife here didn't make us any reservations. Where can we stay until the next plane?"

The Asian stood up and described a stone house at the river's edge. "No hotel but the house is good. The priest there has a key. He let you sleep somewhere."

Walker got another beer and we left the hunter and the Indian on their stools. "It's going to be all right, Beautiful." He kissed me on the neck. "I feel good."

*

WE followed the faint roar of the river and soon came to a large European house. A man in khaki shorts and a black T-shirt with a clerical collar stood in the shadow of an enormous mango tree. "Hello, fellow pilgrims," he called.

"A priest and a fruitcake," Walker said under his breath. "What luck."

I introduced myself.

"The Indian sent you?"

"Yes."

"It's too hot inside. Sit here."

We sat on crumbling steps that led to a high veranda encircling the house. The priest immediately began to talk, as if he were continuing a conversation that had been momentarily interrupted.

"I come here to be peaceful," he said. "I love the Bora, a real

African river, beautiful and deceptive. The Victoria Falls are spectacular and draw the tourists, especially the British, but the Bora here is one of the people's rivers. It gives what it has and it takes what it needs."

Walker lit a cigarette and tried to give it to me, but I shook my head. I didn't like to smoke in front of clergy.

"I'll take that," the priest said.

Walker raised his eyebrows and handed it over. I had to laugh. We'd have a fine time in Gebele. I seldom liked missionaries but the priest had a simplicity that drew me to him. He spoke easily and asked no questions and offered no advice. Walker still looked like a high-strung stock broker, with just the top button of his shirt undone and his body lean and handsome as a cheetah. The priest had the ruddy, creased look of a man who was often smiling and seldom clean-shaven.

"You can sleep on the veranda. It will be cool," the priest said and left us.

I opened my bag, changed into a pair of shorts and opened Walker's suitcase. He lit a cigarette off the one he just finished and threw the butt under the mango tree.

"Are you going like that?" I said.

"Going? Where's to go? I thought this was it."

I still wanted the adventure. "Well, we have to explore, go where we haven't gone before. Don't you want to see my albino?"

"It's two hundred degrees here and nobody but a Dutch priest and a broken-down big game hunter even speak our language. It's too hot to move." He unbuttoned his shirt and pulled it out of his pants. "There is only one place I'm able to go — there," he said, flicking an ash towards the river.

A path from the town lead to the shore of the river just north of the house and several women were gathered there, washing clothes and collecting water. The near side of the river was green; in several places the banks were overgrown with bushes and trees; there was also a wide, sandy beach. On the far side of the river, tall grass stretched to the horizon. The current seemed to be a steady rumble.

"We'll go swimming." He called into the darkness of the priest's room: "We're going swimming in the river, Father. Will our bags be okay here?"

The priest came to the doorway. "Of course, my children. Everything is safe here. But the river, remember the Bora is an African river."

*

THE water was cool and swift. I waded up to my knees and turned to Walker. "What about schistosomiasis?"

"I don't see any snails." He dove in, splashing me with his feet.

The current seemed too fast to carry disease. Walker swam around me, teasing, playing, nibbling at my ankles. Then he lay on his back in the shallows and dozed with his sunglasses on. Around the bend the women washing clothes laughed and chattered and pointed at us. I stretched out beside my husband and watched him sleep. He was tense even when he slept, but eventually the movement of warm water across his body relaxed his muscles and he sank deeper in the sand. The afternoon became slow, peaceful, heavy.

I drifted off, too, until I heard a sharp animal cry. Downstream, a small man in blue shorts tied a goat to a tree in a trampled clearing at the edge of the river, chanted to the animal, and slit its throat. The bleating stopped.

"Walker, did you see that?"

He lifted his head. "Don't look," he said and closed his eyes again.

I leaned on my elbow and watched the man bleed the goat, holding it over a hollowed-out gourd, and then he cut the meat from the skin. A woman took away the fresh meat and the man scraped the skin, rocking and singing as he worked.

"I've never seen anything killed," I said.

"Isn't it part of the adventure?" he said. "Or don't you like it real?"

I lay back in the shallows. He was right, I thought. I'd come to Ethiopia to be entertained; he'd come because he was black and Africa was home.

"You wanted a lot from this year, didn't you?" I said. "I mean it's not an adventure when you care so much."

He found my hand under the water and held it for a long time, then he rolled over on one elbow. His sunglasses fell in the water. He fished them out and dangled them over me so that the water dropped on my face.

"Hey, stop that," I laughed.

"Did I ever tell you about going to the prostitute?"

His words were so unexpected and hard that I cried out.

I don't think he noticed. He lay back in the water and took my hand again. "I took my shirt off and she called in two other women and they surrounded me, giggling and talking behind their fingers. I shouted at them and they flew up chirping like birds and disappeared."

I lay there, crying with my eyes closed, and listened to him dribble clumps of sand in the water. I licked my salty lips.

"I don't think they'd seen a black ferengie before. They were trying to see if I was the same color all over."

I sat up, trembling, and wrapped my towel around my shoulders. "Why in hell are you telling me this? You hurt me easily enough without bragging about prostitutes." I dug my hands in the sand and looked away.

He touched my back with a wet finger. "I'm not trying to hurt you, but don't you see. I'm a freak, a sideshow display. I thought I'd blend in, be part of a majority culture for once in my life, but I'm white as you are here, a ferengie or some sort of half albino." I turned towards him and he smiled. "Everything I do hurts."

Then he stood up, slowly brushed the wet sand off each leg and walked into the river. He was in waist deep water when he looked back. "I'll meet you at that rock in the middle." He dived in and disappeared.

I stood up. There was a boulder the size of a large raft two thirds of the way across the river. I felt a terrible grip on my throat but I couldn't turn away from him. When it was hard to see his head and arms in the dark water, I dove in. The current was faster than it appeared and I had to swim intently for several minutes so I wouldn't be swept downstream. The water roared in my ears. When I finally pulled myself up on the rock, Walker wasn't there. I walked the length of the little island, searching for his black head. I didn't see him. I thought he must be swimming under water, hiding, playing with me. I was out of breath and angry, panting and running back and forth on the rock. I looked back to shore, expecting to find him standing in the shallows, laughing at me for being so easily deceived. He wasn't there — just a lone woman, washing clothes. I looked upstream again. The water was disturbed, flowing around something just beneath the surface. I watched the spot. The swirl widened and the object broke water.

It was Walker's arm, just his forearm from the elbow to the hand. The arm lay limp on the water for ten seconds, twenty seconds, and then I saw the rest of the arm and the nose of a crocodile. I screamed and he was pulled down. The water rushed over the spot and the swirl lengthened and I began to lose the place where I had seen his arm.

I ran to the end of the rock. I heard him telling me about the prostitute again and couldn't get my breath. I couldn't think what to do. "Walker," I shouted. "Walker."

The woman on shore was gathering her wet clothes. I waved at her but she didn't see me and couldn't hear me over the noise of the river. I began to shake, my teeth chattering, freezing in the sun. The woman was getting ready to leave and I had to stop her. There was nowhere else to go, so I slid into the river and swam towards the shore.

When I pulled myself out of the water, the woman looked up. I stared at her, my mouth cupping like a fish breathing poison air. She seemed to guess what had happened and let out a high-pitched wail, throwing down her wash. Another woman appeared and another and they tried to lead me back to the stone house with the high veranda.

"No," I shouted, pulling away from them. "No. My husband is there. Help me."

The women looked at me blankly.

"Get help," I shrieked. I grabbed the arm of the woman nearest me. "Do something." She touched my shoulder with her hand and shook her head. I dropped her arm and turned back to the river. I couldn't leave. I paced up and down, shouting Walker's name at the water, but the river rushed past as if nothing had happened.

Finally the priest came down and I tried to tell him, and he said something to me that I couldn't understand. The women dried me with Walker's towel. I lifted my arms, turned around for them, bent my head so they could rub my hair. The priest told me to go back to the house, that he would get help, and I obeyed.

I remember taking off my wet shorts and shirt and putting on a clean dress and my arms and hands being so heavy. I was sobbing as I tried to dress myself, my body jerking and trembling. When I was finally ready, I ran outside again, down to the edge of the river to look for Walker. I knew that if I could see him again, part of him, I could save him this time. Just give me his hand and I would pull him out. I was the only person who could save him. I paced there until it was dark and I could see the eyes of the women standing around me and then the priest came and led me back to the house. It was hot. He gave me beer and rice and called me his child. People started to gather outside the house.

"An Anuak girl was taken last month," the priest said, "washing clothes just there." He stood at the screen and pointed to a grassy spot on the shore.

"And you didn't tell us?" I went to the edge of the porch and pressed my face against the screen. People swarmed across the yard, their voices buzzing in unfamiliar languagues.

"They are waiting for the hunter," the priest said. "Now that a ferengie is gone, he will kill the crocodile for them." He got up and stood beside me. "I should have told you about the girl."

I moved away. I couldn't stand the sight of him. "What you're saying is that you killed Walker."

"No," he said. "God moves in mysterious ways . . ."

"Don't give me that, you priest," I sobbed. "You killed him. You killed my husband."

"I told you it was an African river," he said. "I thought you understood the danger, my child."

"I'm not anybody's child." I pushed my fingers into my ears, closed my eyes, and leaned into the screen. When I straightened up, the priest was gone.

A woman outside began to chant with the full throat of a gospel singer, beating out a rhythm with her hands. Another woman wailed in a different key. Another and another lifted their voices, wailing and flailing their bodies with their hands. I found the cries in my own throat impossible to keep down and went out under the mango tree to be with them. The women surrounded me and held me up and I wailed and beat my chest with them. Later, asleep somewhere, I dreamed of the white palms of their hands touching me.

*

IN THE MORNING the priest made me write it on a piece of paper first so they could send the telegram in English. My arm shook so violently that I had to grip the pen with both hands to keep it moving and on the page. " 'To AMERICAN EMBASSY, ADDIS ABABA. AMERICAN TEACHER WALKER LUCAS KILLED BY CROCODILE YESTERDAY. Stop' What else do I say?"

"A plane doesn't come for four more days. We can't keep a body in this heat without burying it."

"SEND HELP."

The priest sat with me outside the telecommunications hut all day. The unit was only able to receive messages from one to one-fifteen. I told the priest to go, but he stayed. I was grateful to him for not talking. I twisted my hair around my fingers, making knots, pulling it until my eyes watered; I made designs in the earth with my toes; I smoked all of Walker's cigarettes.

"I've heard his voice all day," I said, finally. "Not words, but the timbre of his voice, speaking too quietly for me to understand."

The priest reached for my hand, but I pulled it away.

"During the war, I was a young man in Holland," he said. "We lived in the country and had a deep cellar where we kept meat and potatoes, turnips and a radio — a forbidden radio.

"I loved a girl with hair yellow like yours. She helped my mother in the summer — we had a large farm. We were to be married. One day my father, my brother, and I were in the fields when we heard shots. We dropped our tools and ran. By the time we got to the house, they were all dead in the yard, my mother, my two sisters, the girl I loved, and the radio had also been shot, blown up."

He touched my arm. "Why these things happen, we don't know. Maybe God knows. I could not speak for two days. And I still dream some nights that it was a mistake, that it didn't happen."

I put my head in my hands. "It's my fault. I made him come here." The priest touched my back and I jerked away, then looked at him. "You think it could be a mistake?"

He shook his head, but he's right, I thought. It's a mistake. Maybe Walker's hiding somewhere, teasing me.

Later, he said, "You know the white hunter shot the crocodile early this morning."

"Yes."

"The Anuak wouldn't cut open the crocodile. It was the biggest they'd ever seen, about five meters. The hunter refused and so the old Asian . . ." He smiled at me. "I don't think Gupta had ever been more than six hundred paces from his stool before." The Asian had slit open the belly of the crocodile and lifted my husband out in pieces.

There was no answer at one o'clock. We sent another cable and walked back to the stone house. Now there would be nothing for twenty-four hours.

*

I WAS washing my hair when I heard people shouting and running. I looked up from the small stream I was standing in, my hair parted in front of my face to keep the soap out of my eyes. It looked as if the whole town were descending on me. A plane, they said, an airplane.

What plane? I ducked my head in the water again and swirled it around. Visions of my grandmother washing my hair at the kitchen sink came to me. I felt the bony hand on the back of my neck, holding me under. If I didn't go back, it wouldn't be true. Walker was hiding some place.

When I came up, rinsed, women stood watching me. I don't know what they said but the sound of their voices and their hard hands propelled me toward the house in a dream. Maybe Walker is waiting on the priest's porch, laughing at me, hiding like he did at the landing strip when the plane left. That was it, I thought. He couldn't stand to be in a place without a train station and so his disappearing act was an elaborate ruse to go home early. He would be there, waiting. I floated up to the house.

The priest had packed our bags. He carried Walker's suitcase as we walked to the landing strip. The path was lined with people. I saw the albino standing apart from the others at the corner of the runway, wrapped in his shamma. I raised my hand in his direction, but he turned away. The priest followed me into the plane.

"Are you coming too?"

"No," he said, "just tucking you in." A refitted cargo plane had been diverted from its scheduled route to pick us up. The seats were backed up along the walls of the plane so the passengers faced each other across the aisle.

A boy stared at me and whispered to his mother, "Ferengie?" The woman nodded and closed her hand over her son's mouth.

"Where's Walker?"

The priest pointed to a square crate tied to two seats in the tail of the plane. "God be with you."

"He's too late," I said.

The priest squeezed my shoulder, then backed out of the plane.

I twisted to look out the window behind me as we took off, but the seat belt held me forward. I only glimpsed the tidy streets of the village and the Bora River curving protectively around it.

Graven Images

THE TWENTY-FIVE DOLLARS OPAL EARNED cleaning the preacher woman's house Mondays wasn't enough. "They'll have to pay me way more'n this if there's stuff going on," she muttered, folding hot jeans at the dryer in the basement. She wrestled with the pants to pull the legs right side out and felt a bulge in the front pocket. "Oh, Lord, not another letter."

She looked over her shoulder at the empty basement, then pinched the envelope with two fingers and slid it out of the pocket. The man's name was written in faint purple ink. "I don't want no part of their problems." She jammed it back. "I ain't giving her another one."

Opal wiped her face with her apron and remembered how white the woman went when she saw the first letter. "What kind of man is he — and her a preacher?" Opal shook her head. "Painting pictures and getting your name in the paper don't give a man leave to cheat on his wife. It make me sick."

After she folded the clothes, she swept the floor. "I'm not going up there until one of 'em leaves. I don't need all that hollering." She could hear the preacher's voice, high and shrill. "Wonder what she sound like in the pulpit with her high woman's voice — it ain't right, a woman trying to preach." She raised her eyes to the ceiling. " 'Let your women keep silent in the churches,' the Bible say."

When she finished the floor, there was nothing left to do in the basement. "I ain't going up there." She pushed the laundry basket aside and hefted herself onto the table, inching backward to lean against the wall, and sat with her legs stretched out. She couldn't find any place to rest her arms and her massive breasts pressing on her belly made her feel like she was wearing a body girdle. She closed her eyes and let her head droop to her shoulder. Least Henry never hollered at me like that man do her, she thought.

When she finally heard the screen door to the kitchen slam, she slid off the table. "Man ought to fix that door. Latch don't hold."

Breathing hard, she carried the laundry through the kitchen past the woman hunched over a coffee cup, smoking a cigarette. Opal didn't say anything and the preacher never looked up. On the second floor, putting away socks, Opal muttered, "The body's a temple and that preacher woman is smoking." She slammed a dresser drawer shut. "I'm going to ask for more money."

When she carried the empty basket downstairs, the preacher was bent over the sink, splashing water on her face with one hand and groping for a towel with the other. Her gray hair was damp at the hairline and stood in soft peaks around her face. She wore jeans and a sweat shirt that swallowed her slight figure, making her look like a farm wife. This woman don't look like no minister of the gospel, Opal thought.

"I'm going for a bike ride, Opal, up in the hills. If anyone calls, I'm not available today."

"Yes, ma'am."

She unplugged the coffee pot and cleared the table. The preacher slammed the back door, then returned with a red plastic bottle that said Fuji on the side. She opened the refrigerator, took out a box of wine, filled the red bottle, and shoved the box back in the refrigerator.

"Good-bye, Opal." She let the screen door flop on the frame.

Opal pushed eggs and bacon through the garbage disposal. She turned it on and stood at the door to watch the preacher mount her bike and ride away. "Smoking first, and now liquor. I ain't staying in this place," Opal said and switched off the disposal

*

SHE was vacuuming the living room carpet when the man came. She turned her back to him and stooped to clean under the sofa. The vacuum went dead, she straightened up and he was standing two feet away, holding the plug in his hand.

"I can't talk over that thing. Where's Eva?"

Opal put on her stupid look.

"My wife. Where's my wife?"

"Riding a bicycle."

He nodded his head like he understood something. "I brought my van, Opal. I want you to help me load some things from the studio."

She shook her head. "No, sir, I got a lot of work to do," she nodded at the room, "and you know I don't go up them stairs."

The man swung the cord and looked around the room, smiling and bobbing his head. He seemed excited. Opal looked out the picture window and saw a tall, blond woman standing by the van, staring at her reflection in the side mirror. She was wearing shorts and high-heeled sandals. She glanced toward the house and Opal got a flash of full, red lips. You point your harlot mouth the other way, girl. I seen women like you before, she thought. The woman turned back to the mirror and Opal faced the man.

"I don't know if I can make it in one trip, Opal. I'll bring everything down to the first floor and you can help me carry it out to the van."

She fiddled with the vacuum cleaner, adjusting the bag. "I don't carry heavy things. Doctor told me that."

The man frowned and looked out the window at the woman. "All right, Opal, all right. I'll do it myself." He plugged in the vacuum.

He removed pictures from the walls and took sculpture from the mantle. As soon as Opal finished polishing the coffee table, he carried it out. "I made it."

Opal decided to wash the picture window. She watched the girl help him load the van. He took off his flannel shirt and put it on the girl. The shirt was so big on her that it covered her shorts and made her look like she was naked underneath. The man kissed her on the nose and she climbed in the front seat of the van. "A man like you make me sick," Opal said and spat on the window. When she heard him at the door, she sprayed the glass with Windex and rubbed hard.

Inside, he leaned on the banister. "I made this house beautiful, didn't I, Opal?" The walls were bare and there were circles and rectangles imprinted in the carpet where he had removed sculpture and furniture. She didn't say anything.

"I made it into something. Eva has no sense of space or form." He seemed to be waiting for Opal to speak. "Give the reverend my new phone number and tell her I didn't get the studio cleaned out. She's not to touch it." He handed her a card with a number on it. "I'll be back Sunday morning to finish up. She won't have to see me."

*

OPAL ate lunch by herself at the kitchen table, tuna salad on whole wheat toast and skim milk. Then she went upstairs to change the sheets on the bed and clean the bedroom and bathroom. His clothes weren't in the closet and the only pictures left on the walls were photographs.

She was scouring the bathroom sink when she heard the kitchen door bang.

"Opal . . . Opal?" It was the preacher. She put the Ajax away and went downstairs, her hand heavy on the railing.

The woman stood in the middle of the living room with one hand on her hip, the other squeezing the red bottle that said Fuji. "What happened here? Where is everything?" She was flushed and sweaty and her voice was thin.

Opal looked over the woman's head, but didn't answer until she was off the last step and in the living room. "Your husband came, Ma'am."

The woman stared for a minute. "The slime rat." She threw the red bottle on the sofa. It bounced on the floor and hit her shoe. "Damn his lizard eyes." She grabbed the bottle and flung it against the wall. "I'll crush that cockroach and fry him." She hurled a pillow at the window and raised her fist at Opal. "I'll kill him."

Opal took a step backward, her head moving side to side like an old grandma at a revival meeting. She clasped her hands together. "Preacher, you shouldn't talk like that. 'Forgive and ye shall be forgiven.' Luke six, thirty-seven."

The woman pointed a pillow at Opal. "Are you quoting scripture to me?"

"Yes, ma'am."

The preacher threw back her head and paced the length of the room. "Oh, boy, that's great, that's really great. . .just great." She slung the pillow, knocking over a lamp.

Opal rubbed the backs of her hands, one after another, and felt sick to her stomach. "Preacher, remember the Bible says 'But love ye your enemies and do good.' "

The woman raised a hand to stop her. "I know, Luke again and don't call me preacher." She wiped her face as if she'd stumbled into a spider web. "I feel like killing him." She paused. "If he were here, I'd kill him."

Opal nodded and looked away, rubbing her chest to keep her heart from pressing against her lungs. She knew what it was to feel like killing a man. She took a deep breath to block out the woman's words. There was work to be done.

"He hurt me." The woman dropped down on the sofa and covered her face with her hands, crying silently. "You have no idea. I feel so stupid."

Opal didn't want to talk, but the woman wouldn't stop crying. We ought to pray, she thought, but she said, "I know how it is."

The woman looked up.

"I know," Opal said again. "It's like he done stabbed you all over with a rusty, twisting knife and then broke off the handle, leaving the blade inside to fester and rot. It's like he don't see nothing but his own face in a mirror. Man wants the tight feel of money in his pocket and the tight ass of some new woman and . . ." Opal caught herself and snatched the dust cloth from her lap. She stood up, pushing her hand against her chest, and began to polish an end table.

"Are you married, Opal?"

"Was."

She finished dusting the table.

"Henry — that's his name — walks in the kitchen one Saturday morning, early — I'm washing the breakfast dishes — he's holding the baby. He hand the child to me and say he going to Florida. Say he can't breathe in my house."

"I can't stand it."

The woman threw another pillow across the room. "Max said the same thing — no air to breathe." She addressed the floor. "He says that because of what's her name, he can work. That an artist has to have inspiration and he can't get it here." She dropped her voice in imitation of her husband. " 'You're too serious. Lighten up. We never should have gotten married in the first place.' " The woman looked at Opal. "We've been married fifteen years and he says it was all a mistake. He says that marriage doesn't mean anything — that I took it all too seriously."

Opal could see the back of Henry's head in the shine of the table she was polishing. He had said marriage was a joke and took a high-breasted girl to Florida with him.

The woman was crying again. "I'm supposed to know how to handle this. I'm a minister, damn it. What am I going to do? I feel so ugly."

She wiped her eyes and got out a little laugh. " 'Vanity of vanities, sayeth the preacher, all is vanity.' Did you know that even a forty-year-old woman wants her husband to think she's cute?" She wrinkled her nose to adjust her glasses. Her eyes were red and her face was pale as an early moon. "How can I compete with a woman half my age?"

Opal dusted the table in slow circles, watching her own scaly hand with the split fingernails bitten to the quick. She remembered the way she used to file those nails long and sharp and paint them Raven Red. Henry once said she had the sexiest hands in four states. "Do you want to pray, Ma'am?"

The woman looked startled. "Oh, no, not now." She took off her glasses and wiped her eyes with the front of her sweat shirt. "Just not right now. I'm sorry, Opal. I have to think."

"Thinking don't help. That make it worse, to try to make sense out of it," said Opal. "I asked Henry what I done wrong and he said nothing . . . I done nothing at all. He just say he tired of my face and left. I felt like some old pair of boots kicked in the corner. He used me up and left." She polished the same spot over and over.

The woman watched her work. "How long ago?"

"Five years." Opal stopped polishing. "I cook his dinner, iron his clean shirt, sleep in his bed every night, and then he left me."

The woman went to the kitchen and brought back a box of tissues. "When Max and I were first married," she said, "he used to tell me that when I turned forty, he'd trade me in for two twenties. It was a big joke." She pushed her hair back with both hands and looked at Opal. "I guess that's what he's done, isn't it?"

"Yes, Ma'am, it is." Opal thought of her three children around the dinner table every night, arguing and talking about school, laughing and teasing her. Henry don't have that. He don't have nothing. "I was scared at first but men ain't everything, Ma'am. We getting along at my house. A man ain't everything."

The woman sat with her arms resting on her knees, staring out the picture window. She had stopped crying. The yellow maple on the boulevard reflected a light that spread across the room like the diffused sunlight on the cover of a Sunday School text. Opal rubbed a dirty spot on the window with a corner of her apron, then put the pillows back on the sofa and sat down next to the woman.

After a while, the woman said, "What time did he come?"

"About eleven."

"Was he alone?"

"She didn't come in the house."

The woman turned away and said something Opal couldn't hear.

"He brought a big van."

"Did he say anything to you?"

"Nothing much. He ask me to help carry, but I say I can't."

"That's all?"

"He say he be back Sunday morning to finish in the studio and he left his phone number on a card. I put it on the refrigerator."

"His phone number? That was fast." The woman stared at the floor, her head bobbing slowly, moving closer and closer to her knees.

They sat without speaking again. Opal let her head touch the soft upholstery and closed her eyes. She saw Henry in that dream she had, laid out and shameless in his black suit and red tie on a white satin pillow. She wished he were dead so she could forget about him. She shook her head to slough off the old feelings, then leaned on the arm rest to get up.

The woman put out her hand to keep her. "Did he say anything else, anything at all?"

"He ask where you were and I told him."

The woman nodded. "What else?"

"He say he make the house beautiful." Opal spoke carefully. "He say it was hard to work here."

The woman looked at her sharply. "Did he say I have no sense of space or form?"

Opal nodded. "I better be getting to my work."

The woman slung another pillow across the room. "That cross-eyed weasel."

She looked around for something else to throw, then got up. Standing there, in the middle of the half-empty living room, the woman reminded Opal of a picture she saw once of a girl in a corn field with the stalks bent and broken. Her eyes held light the same way.

"All right. Let's get to work. We've got work to do in the studio."

"Ma'am, he say not to touch the studio," Opal said.

"I'm sure he did. Come on, Opal."

"It ain't my place to clean that studio." Opal dabbed at a lamp shade with her rag.

The woman grabbed her hand. "I'll pay you extra. This has to be done now."

Opal tried to hold back but the woman pulled her up the two flights of stairs so suddenly that she could hardly move her feet fast enough and she had to lean against the wall at the top to catch her breath. The woman opened the door and flicked the light switch. Half the roof was glass and spotlights shot out of the corners. Opal shielded her eyes. The room was filled with shapes and bright colors — hunks of iron and sparkling mounds of plaster that looked like unfinished sand castles. Covering one wall was a painting of women cut off at the waist. They were bending or twisting or pointing straight ahead — black women, white, brown and all of them naked. Opal chewed her lip and surveyed the room slowly. In a corner was a thing that looked like a woman's breast. She narrowed her eyes and shook her head. "What you want me to do, Ma'am."

"Open the windows to the back and take off the screens. We're going to throw all this stuff out."

"Out the windows? That sound crazy."

"Good. You just open those windows."

The woman dragged the breast over. "I hate this . . . this tit," she said and forced it through the open window. Opal hauled over a rusted piece of iron that was curved like an anchor at one end and flared like a crow's wing at the other. The woman pushed it out. The point of the anchor pierced the giant breast and foam and plaster spewed over the back yard.

"Did you see that?" The woman's eyes were wide and bright and she stared into the yard. She put her arm around Opal, smiling. " 'Thou shalt not make unto thee any graven image or any likeness of anything that is in the heaven above," Opal pulled away, "or that is in the earth beneath, or that is in the waters under the earth.' "

Opal blinked like gnats were swarming round her face. "I don't think we ought to be doing this, Ma'am. I'd just as soon carry this stuff down the back stairs."

"Don't worry, Opal. The neighbors can't see us. Just haul the rest of that garbage over here."

"No, Ma'am, it's not the neighbors." Sweat stood on Opal's face like rain drops and she felt dizzy and her stomach twisted inside her. "Heaving stuff out like this don't seem right. Everything's all breaking up."

"Exactly. 'Thou shalt not commit adultery.' Keep heaving."

*

THEY worked without a break, the woman pointing and Opal hauling pictures and sculpture over to the window. The woman was thin-lipped and sweaty and her tears left squiggly lines in the dirt on her face, but after a while it all looked like sweat. She whooped and quoted scripture everytime she shoved something through the window. " 'Man that is born of woman is full of trouble.' " She dropped a half-finished carving that looked like a bouquet of women's hands. " 'A time to kill,' " and she hurled a chisel after the painting of the naked women.

Opal's nausea passed and she felt light-headed. " 'The soul that sinneth, it shall die.' " She handed the woman an unfinished painting of a tree with human limbs for branches penciled in.

"Good, Opal, very good."

The last piece was a huge parrot with blue and gold feathers glued to a canvas of trees. The woman couldn't get the bird through the window. "Get me that saw, Opal." She sliced the front off the bird, pushed both pieces out and flung the saw after them. " 'Joy to the just.' "

The room was empty. They stood together at the window staring down into the backyard.

"Oh, Opal, what have we done?"

The small yard looked like a cemetery that had been backhoed.

Iron, wood, fake body parts and metal strips filled the yard so that only patches of grass were visible.

"Ma'am, you crazy."

"Thank you, Opal. Thank you. Say that again."

Opal grinned. "You plumb crazy, Preacher." She leaned out the window to get a better look. "Now who you think's going to clean up that mess?"

"I'll call Max at his new number and tell him I loosened up a little and moved his art to the back yard." She straightened her sweat shirt with exaggerated dignity. "I'll insist that he get his things out of here immediately. He doesn't have to wait until the Sabbath to do his dirty work." She slammed her hand on the wall. "It's quite a sight, isn't it, Opal?" She held her head like she was crying, but when she looked up, she was gasping and snickering. She started to laugh out loud and put her arm around Opal.

"Did you see the perfect tit explode? Too bad Max wasn't lying across it."

Opal shook her head at the thought and started to laugh. Soon the two of them were laughing so hard that they had to hold on to the wall and each other to keep from falling.

"It's just art." The woman could hardly talk, she was wiping her eyes and laughing. "It doesn't mean anything, he always says. Everything doesn't have significance. I don't have to be so damn serious, do I?" She linked her arm through Opal's and waved her hand at the room. "Now what?"

"Well," said Opal. "I'll do the floor. It's filthy up here."

She got the mop and the woman carried up a pail of hot soapy water. "You can wax it next week when you come. But get it clean as sin today." She paused at the door. "We had quite a day, didn't we, Opal?"

Opal nodded and hummed to herself, swirling the mop in the clean water. She would do the walls next week, rub out the rectangles where art used to hang.

Natural Causes

ABBY TELLS FORREST SHE'S LEAVING HIM the morning after he's killed her cat. He says it's a stupid reason because he didn't really kill the cat. The cat died of natural causes.

"Oh, yeah," Abby says. "You call freezing to death under the azalea bush natural causes?"

"What was not natural was having that animal in the house." He stubs out his cigarette in a saucer and leaves the dead butt there. Abby hates cigarettes and especially hates them left on plates that people use.

"And she didn't freeze to death," he says. "The cat was old. It was her time."

"She probably got a broke leg when you threw her out the door last night," Abby says. "You try explaining it to the kids."

Forrest is reading *TV Guide*. He keeps his finger at his place and looks up. "Anything, man or beast, that pees on the floor don't belong in this house."

Abby takes his saucer and puts an ash tray down. "You're stinking up my kitchen. Smoke don't belong in here, neither. Go on outside," she says. "If it weren't too cold for that cat, it's not too cold for you."

She drops the saucer in the sink and ties an apron that says "Kiss the Cook" over her bathrobe. She pulls on rubber gloves and starts to wash the dishes. The left glove has a hole in it and the hot water seeping up her index finger makes her hand sticky. A bowl slips out of her hand, sending a wave of suds down her neck and apron. Warm water slides down her chest bone, between her breasts, and spreads over her belly and she feels peculiar, like she might faint or throw up. She leans on the counter for a minute, eyes closed, then turns to Forrest to tell him she's sick. He's angled against the wall, the two legs of his chair jammed in the linoleum, digging up floor wax, as he drinks coffee, smokes, and reads the TV listings under his breath.

"You're going to snap those chair legs," she says and the bowl slips out of her hand and hits the floor.

Forrest doesn't move.

"Dang stupid bowl," Abby says and kicks the bowl into the cupboard.

"Better watch your language, Abby. The kids'll hear you." He laughs.

"You got nerve to say that to me. You look like the King of Siam sitting there," she says. "Can I bring you anything, your highness . . . more coffee?"

He leans forward and the chair wobbles and bounces on the floor. "Hey, I want you to watch Channel 8 at noon today," he says. "They've got a program on Dahlonega and the gold mining. We stopped there on the way home from Gatlinburg that time — remember?"

She jerks the sink stopper out and the soapy water disappears, sucking and swirling. She remembers that trip to Tennessee. She remembers the three kids arguing nonstop in the back seat and she remembers that she was sick to her stomach and scared to death that they were going to fall off one of those mountain roads. She remembers feeling wrinkled and tired all the time and eating in dirty little restaurants. She remembers people staring at them, at her especially, wearing a house dress — her mama didn't raise her to wear shorts and sandals in town. She remembers the first day in that tourist trap — the kids walking so close that she felt like they were glued to her at the heel. Then they got used to the neon glitz of the streets and took off without her. What really got her was Chris Ann paying a dollar for a grab bag surprise that turned out to be a wooden paddle with a ball on a rubber band worth twenty-five cents and then being happy about it, until Abby called it a piece of junk. "Ma, you spoil everything," Chris Ann said. Abby felt cheated and out of place the whole week and she didn't leave the house for days after they got home.

"That was the best time this family ever had," Forrest says, laughing. "Wonder where that gold nugget Willie found is now. Do you remember how he carried on when he saw that thing in his pan?"

"You know I can't stand for you to talk about Willie. Why do you do me that way?" Abby slams a can of Ajax on the counter and glares at Forrest.

He is smiling. "Ain't no harm in remembering the good times, Baby," he says.

"Don't 'Baby' me. I don't have time for remembering," Abby says, sprinkling cleanser in the sink. "I got stuff to do, Forrest. I told you, I'm leaving."

Forrest lifts an eyebrow, drops his cigarette butt in his coffee cup, then pushes his cup aside and turns on the TV.

"Did you hear me?" she says, raising her voice. "I'm leaving you — as soon as I can."

Forrest has found a Road Runner cartoon and is hunched forward, adjusting the color. He puts a lot of red in the picture when he watches cartoons.

She pulls the rubber gloves off inside out and smacks them on the edge of the sink. "I'm leaving you. It's all over." She is talking to the kitchen window, her back to him. Since William left, she has avoided looking straight at him. He has the same wild, curly hair and square jaw as his son and it hurts Abby to look at him. He's too much like Willie.

Forrest turns the sound down. "You just need to get out of the house more, Abby. You don't see people enough. Why don't you talk to Olive about sewing?" She turns around and he turns up the sound on the TV. The Road Runner has just disappeared in a whirlwind of dust and the coyote sprawls pointing in four directions in the middle of the road.

*

" 'DON'T be surprised if I'm not here when you get back' is what I said to him when he left for work," Abby tells Olive. "I even told Buddy to go straight to James's after school."

Olive is appliqueing a yellow duck and four ducklings on a white sweat shirt. The mother duck holds an umbrella under embroidered rain drops. She stops her machine. "What did he say when you told him you were leaving?"

Abby starts to cry. "He said he'd drop me at a bar, buy me the first drink and I'd die of thirst before anybody'd buy me the second. Then he laughed and told me to have a nice day." She wipes her eyes with the backs of her hands. "I don't want to be there when he comes home and I got nowhere to go. He don't listen to me."

"You got any money?"

Abby shakes her head.

"Then what you need, woman, is a job."

"I don't know how to do anything."

"Hell, Abby, you can cook, you can clean, you can raise young'uns. You can fix things. You're plenty smart."

Abby sits up straighter, feeling hopeful. "Well, I'm not going to be no maid at thirty-six," she says.

"Go home, get the paper and start reading those want ads." Olive gets up and takes Abby by the elbow. "Come on. Go get something for yourself. Like I got my appliqueing here and all the craft shows — my own money, my own life. Royce don't get none of this. It's time for you to get something for yourself."

*

SHE hasn't looked for a job since she was seventeen years old and just graduated from high school. Her daddy had had the first heart attack and was sitting in the La-Z-Boy with pillows stuffed everywhere. He made her go through the classifieds in the Atlanta Constitution, circling the possibilities. She kept wanting to stop, but he made her read every ad. She only went for one interview, at the dry cleaners on the square in Clintock, and the man said he'd call her but he never did and then her daddy died and Forrest said he was going into his uncle's construction business and that was that. They got married right after her eighteenth birthday.

She crosses out the first ad without finishing it and dials Olive's number. "Olive, what you think I'm going to get a job doing? I don't type and I don't account and I don't read initials — IBM PC W slash P. This ain't for me."

"Keep reading, sugar. Those ads are for everybody — you're there somewhere." Olive hangs up before Abby has a chance to say anything.

After an hour of reading and crossing out, she makes four calls. Two of them want her to come for an interview, a Food Sales and a Waitress job. "Olive, I got nothing to wear."

"Don't move. I'm coming over."

Olive goes through her closet, pulls out her plum pants suit and her flowered shirt waist dress that she bought in Atlanta the last time and a plain black skirt with a turquoise blouse. "There," says Olive triumphantly. "Don't you try to tell me you got nothing to wear. Get dressed and get going."

Abby polishes her black heels, scrubs her nails, and makes the bed. Then she dresses quickly in the black skirt and blouse and pulls her stiff, curly hair into a bun at the nape of her neck. She looks at herself once in the mirror and is surprised: "I'm almost pretty." She smiles at her reflection and turns around slowly. "Oh, Lord," she says, "what am I doing?"

She stops by Olive's house on her way to the bus stop. "Whoa, girl, you look just like a secretary," Olive says.

"I look okay?"

"You look great, honey."

Abby laughs. She remembers her image in the mirror and juts her hip out. "I don't type but typing's not everything, is it?" She bats her eyelashes at Olive and lowers her head. "I think I'm just perfect for the job."

Olive swats her with a dish towel and pushes her out the door. "Get going, woman, and just remember what kind of job you're after."

Abby stops on the porch. "I feel like I'm running away from something," she says. "Listen, Olive, I don't want to be home when Forrest gets there. I'll call Buddy at James's house after school and tell him just to stay. I want that house empty when Forrest walks in — no supper, no children, no wife — just him and a freshly buried cat." She laughs and shakes her head. "Sounds like something a kid would do, hiding, but if he asks you, you don't know nothing."

"Right," Olive says. "Now go, woman."

She doesn't look back until she gets to the bus stop.

*

IT'S 8:30 at night when Abby steps off the bus at the fork in the road. She picks her way along the gravel shoulder, trying not to scuff her shoes, and takes deep breaths, looking down towards her house, to see if there are any lights on. She can't tell if the house is lit up or not. She passes Olive's house and sees the shine of the TV screen in the window and Olive sitting in the living room with Royce. Her own house looks dark. She's halfway up the driveway before she notices Forrest sitting on the front steps, the red glow of his cigarette flickering like a firefly.

"Where the hell have you been?" he says and throws the cigarette into the yard. A car passes on the highway and the headlights throw the image of his hand up against the white house, the shadow swooping like a hunting bird. He's not a big man but he has massive hands − one can cover her whole face, and he used to pick her up by spreading his hands tight around her waist. She has a flash of him holding William in the hospital − the newborn baby disappearing in his two hands. "And where's the children?" he says.

She stops where she is. "Buddy is over to James's," she says. "I told him you'd pick him up later, and Chris Ann has been at your Mama's all week. She don't come home 'til Saturday." She adjusts her purse on her shoulder. "I assume you aren't asking me about William since you're the one who signed for him." She starts to walk around to the back door.

"Wait a minute, Abby, where you going? Come over here and sit a while with me."

She stops again and shakes her head. "No, I don't think so." She hesitates. "I don't want to get my skirt dirty, sitting on that stoop. I'll see you inside."

She hurries around the house, in the back door, and into the bathroom. She wants to get her things off and think a minute before he comes in from the front porch. She takes her time changing and he's waiting at the kitchen table when she comes out.

"You want to tell me what's going on?" He says this quietly and he doesn't look at her.

She sits down across from him, leaning on her elbows, pressing both hands tightly together. She tries to look straight at him, but can't. "I told you this morning but you weren't listening. I said I'm fixing to leave you — soon, real soon." He raises his head and she looks away.

He covers her hands with a hand that is so hard and calloused it doesn't feel human at all; it feels like an old ragged leather glove that got wet and was left out in the sun and dried to a hard, sharp shape. "This is more than that fool cat, ain't it?"

She nods.

"Abby, I'm a good provider. You got what you need here. I can't see what you're missing." He coughs from deep in his lungs, hard and long. When he can speak again, his face is red and his eyes are rheumy as an old man's. "It ain't another man, is it?"

"No," she says and thinks of William again, the spitting image of his daddy, people always said, but with the heart of his mama. She remembers him and Forrest standing out in the yard, Forrest pitching the ball so it hit William's bat — the four-year-old laughing at the home runs he got. "It's Willie," she says.

He drops her hands. "Ain't nothing we can do about Willie until he decides to pick up a telephone or write a letter. I wish you'd stop acting like joining the Marines was the worst thing that could happen to a boy."

"He is only seventeen and he didn't even tell me he was going," she says, holding her head in her hands. "He never even said goodbye to me."

Forrest stands up suddenly. "He ain't dead, for Crissakes, and I wish you'd quit acting like he was. We got two other children and ourselves to take care of. I come home after a hard day's work, bringing my paycheck" — he pulls it out of his pocket and throws it on the table — "and my house is dark, my wife and children are gone, I got no supper and nobody knows nothing. What I want to know is where the hell have you been?"

"No, he's not dead but you drove him out just the same," she says. "You treated him so harsh. You always picked on him." She folds her arms and turns away.

"I did not pick on my son," he says. He hits the wall behind him with his fist, not too hard but solidly.

She stands up suddenly and leans across the table. "I been scared of you, just like you wanted. You make me feel like nothing, that what I think or feel counts for nothing."

"I never wanted that," he says quietly.

"Well, you could have fooled me," she says, wiping her eyes. "Do you know how often I stood down in that basement hating you while you were hollering at Willie, me scared to come up? You never did Chris Ann or Buddy that way. And then Willie left me without a word, me who always tried to protect him." She is crying and trying to hold back the tears with her fingers.

"Damn it, Abby, Willie had different responsibilities being the first born. You know that." Forrest's voice is far away.

Abby wipes her eyes again but they won't dry. She gets a paper towel and stands at the sink with her back to him. "I guess it don't matter now. He's gone." She takes a deep breath and scrapes at a stain on the counter with her thumb nail. "I got a job. I got a job down at Clintock Mall, selling in a store."

He smacks the table with his open hand. "Oh, no, you don't, Abby," he says. "I won't have that. You got a job here — me and the kids."

"You're the one told me to get out more." She takes a can of chicken noodle soup off the shelf, opens it, and empties it in a sauce pan. "Getting out was a good idea. I saw today I been stupid about a lot of things." She looks at the window and sees her dim outline in the dark glass.

He lights a cigarette and sits down again. Her spoon scrapes and bangs on the saucepan as she stirs the soup. Forrest leans on his elbows at the table, staring at the cigarette as he smokes. After several minutes, he says, "I don't know what you're talking about, Abby."

She turns the soup down to a simmer. "I read the ads in the newspaper today," she says, "and couldn't understand half of them — the dang want ads. You know what WANG is?"

Forrest doesn't say anything.

"Well, it made me want to throw up, made me sick that I could be so ignorant." She ladles the soup into two bowls. "You were right about one thing, Forrest. I got to get out. I got to do more than keep this kitchen floor clean and wait for Willie to call."

"So what if he does call?" says Forrest, looking up. "How're you going to know, down there at the mall?"

The hot soup dribbles over her hand as she sets the bowl in front of him. "I hadn't thought of that," she says.

"There's a lot you haven't thought about. I meant you could do something at home, like Olive. I don't want you going out to work." He hits his hand with his fist and leans across the table. "My daddy always said that a steady job and a good family's all a man needs in this world and that's what I've believed and that's what I've worked for all my life."

She knocks the ladle on the side of the pan and fills the pan with hot water. "Did your daddy say what a woman needs?" she asks.

*

AT Health's Harvest Abby gives her full name, Abigail, and that's what they call her. She learns to run the juicer and make carrot juice, celery juice, beet juice, anything.

"There was a guy today," she tells Buddy, "that came in wanting potato juice. Can you beat that?"

He shakes his head.

"Well, I made it for him and he drunk it down, said it was good and paid me a dollar-fifty for it. I couldn't believe it."

"Did you taste it?" he asks.

"No," she says. "We were too busy."

Abby likes the job. She feels like everything is brand new — the work, the people, the long skirt and bandana that Jake, the manager, gave her to wear. Even the people that come in the store look different.

"They're thinner than we are," she tells Buddy, "and peachier looking."

"You're weird, Mom," he says.

She quits teasing her hair and combs it back into a pony tail. "Mama, that looks sick," Chris Ann tells her.

"This is the natural look, young lady, and it looks a sight better than purple eyes and hot pink cheeks. You could do to let your natural beauty shine through."

Abby scrubs her teeth with baking powder toothpaste and washes her face with a loofa.

"That thing looks like the brush I clean the grill with," Forrest says.

She is still planning to leave him, but she tells him she has to be thoroughly prepared before they start the divorce.

Forrest stops telling funny stories at suppertime and he doesn't come up behind her while she's washing dishes to dig his hands in her pockets and nuzzle her neck. He seems to be watching her, like a cat stalking something, she tells Olive. "Things are better at home. Forrest's not violating my space."

She's learned about personal space from Jake, her manager. She is becoming a whole woman, she feels, developing her inner self at Health's Harvest under Jake's guidance. Jake wears a mustache and a beard, she tells Forrest, because it is so natural.

"You ever think of letting your beard grow?" she asks him one day, as she slices tofu into cubes and sprinkles tamari sauce over them.

He has just come in from the filling station where he works weekends and he looks tired. He drops his boots in the middle of the kitchen floor and sits at the table, drinking a tall glass of tea and smoking a cigarette.

"Why don't you sugar this tea anymore?" he asks. "It don't dissolve right when I have to add it later."

Abby turns to him, hands on her hips. "Do you know how bad sugar is for you? When I think how ignorant we been all these years, the food I gave those children when I didn't know better, I could just throw up. The sugar bowl is out of the house now, I can tell you that."

Forrest stares at her, doesn't say anything until she turns back to the tofu. "Abby, I don't like what's been happening here — you tearing down everything that's ever meant anything to us," he pauses as she turns around, "at least to me, anyways. Nothing satisfies you anymore: the house, the food, the children, me. It's not right."

"Forrest, you're the only thing that doesn't satisfy me and I told you a long time ago what I'm going to do one of these days."

He looks at her, smoking his cigarette in short drags, his fingers near the end. "I didn't make William leave, you know. I jump everytime that phone rings, same as you."

"You signed for him," Abby says. She dumps the tofu and vegetables into a hot frying pan and stirs vigorously with a wooden paddle. "I aim to leave you as soon as I'm ready."

He bangs his fist on the table and the sugar bowl flies off and

breaks on the linoleum. Abby stares at him, shakes her head, and moves to pick up the broken dish.

"Don't touch it," he says.

"But, Forrest . . ."

"Don't touch that bowl," he says again, "and don't talk about leaving any more. I can't stand it."

She holds the wooden spatula, waiting.

"You talk like it's some sort of vacation trip you're going on. I need you here, Abby. The kids need you." He looks at her, his big shoulders hunched around his neck. "I think you look real nice now — your hair and all."

"I hate it when you slam on the table and break things," she says. "Somebody better pick that bowl up before one of the kids comes in here barefoot." She adds the sprouts and stirs again. "It's too late, Forrest. I guess I just don't love you any more. That's all there is to it." She turns on the exhaust fan over the stove.

He drops his cigarette in the iced tea and walks out the back door in his stocking feet. She looks after him, then turns the flame down and sweeps up the sugar and broken glass.

*

JAKE says Abby has a flair for food preparation. The shop starts to sell sandwiches on whole grain bread and plain yogurt with fresh fruit along with the juices. Jake puts Abby in charge of the food counter. He asks her to come early one morning a week to set up, and then increases that to three so they can work together on organizing the menu and placing food orders. The children are in school and, as Abby tells Olive, they can take care of themselves. She catches the bus at 6:55 in the morning. "Forrest could give me a ride, but he says it's in the wrong direction and I ought to be at home anyway, getting the kids off to school." Abby shakes her head. "I tell him that a sixth grader don't need her mama to tell her what to wear or to pour a bowl of cereal and Buddy don't listen to anything I say anyhow."

Abby is trying to help Olive. "You been using that vitamin E cream I gave you?" she asks.

"Oh, a dab now and then," Olive says. "I still got a bunch of Avon to use up."

"That Vitamin E is a miracle substance," Abby says. "It scares me sometimes. Jake says if I use much more of it I'll look like one of my children. Of course, he says he can't hardly believe that I really got such old children, I look so young."

Olive looks at her sharply. "Is there something going on you're not telling me about?"

Abby smiles. "No, honey, there's not, though sometime I wonder . . ." She examines her nails — her hands are her best feature. "I'm still going to leave Forrest soon as I'm ready, and Jake is the sort of man who knows stuff."

"He married?" Olive asks.

Abby nods. "Him and his wife don't get on at all, he says. She doesn't care nothing about her body, and the food she's giving their baby just makes him sick but he can't stop her because he has to provide for the family and can't control what happens when he's not there. I really feel sorry for him."

*

JAKE kisses the back of her neck one morning, before the store opens. The cage is still down, separating them from the mall and the night watchman and the senior citizens who walk every morning from 7:30 to 9:00 to get their exercise. She's rinsing alfalfa sprouts and he kisses her right on the neck. He kind of purrs like a cat when he does it and then tastes her ear. She shakes her head and says, "Hey, what you doing?" but she doesn't move or speak too loudly because there is no wall on the cage and she can see the old people walking out there. He puts his arms around her, spreads his hands over her stomach and kisses her neck again with his mouth open.

"Jake?" she says.

"Oh, you are tasty," he whispers in her ear and moves his hands up to her breasts. She feels her nipples harden in his hands and he holds her tightly, so tightly that she can hardly turn around, but she does and kisses him, too, full on the mouth and there is this little cloud that slides over her brain, like those bubbles of conversation in the comic strips and this one says "What am I doing? I'm a married woman"—and then she remembers that she is going to leave Forrest and the bubble pops and Jake is kissing her and purring like a cat and pulling her back into the store room.

"We have an hour," he says and he pulls her down on the futon that covers the floor of the closet. Abby doesn't remember seeing the futon spread out before.

*

WHEN she gets home from work that night, Forrest is at the stove, frying hamburgers.

"What are you doing?" Abby says.

"What you think I'm doing?" he says. "Cutting the grass?"

"You don't have to be smart with me," she says. "Didn't I tell you what Jake said about the carbon in hamburgers?"

He doesn't say anything, just keeps cooking and after a while Abby goes to change her clothes.

After dinner Chris Ann and Buddy are washing the dishes and Abby sits at the table, filing her nails. Forrest goes out the back door and she can see him hunched over on the steps, the red light of his cigarette traveling from his knee to his mouth and back again. He lights a second cigarette from the first and she calls through the screen, "Those cancer sticks going to kill you."

He finishes the cigarette and stands at the door, looking through the screen. "I got to drive over to see Mama for a minute. These kids can finish up here," he says. "Why don't you come with me?"

She frowns, examining a nail. "I'm kinda busy."

He's waiting for her but doesn't say anything more. He just stands silhouetted in the doorway.

Abby remembers Jake and a tremor runs through her body. She stands up guiltily. "Oh, all right, but I don't want to miss 'Cheers.' We be back by then?"

He opens the screen door for her.

They drive out Applecreek Road in the wrong direction. "Where we going, Forrest? This isn't the way to your mama's."

He turns in at the Methodist campground. The cabins are deserted; in the twilight they all have square black eyes on either side of the doors. There is a sagging pavilion in the middle of the clearing and a couple of tire swings at one end. Forrest and Abby have been there for family reunions and once she went with Olive to a revival meeting. The Methodists will rent it out to anybody.

"I got to talk to you, Abby," he says and stops the car. He turns in his seat to face her and lights a cigarette. "You're talking about leaving me all the time. It's been half a year or more now. I want to know when you're going?"

She feels like he slapped her. "Whew," she says. She flattens her back against the car door and stretches out her hand. "Give me one of those weeds." He hands her his cigarette and lights another one. "You in some kind of a hurry to get rid of me?" She takes a long, slow draw on the cigarette and laughs and coughs at the same time. "Not that it's a problem for me. I'm making good money at Health Harvest — me and the kids can get by."

"You never said nothing about the kids," he says. "I've been thinking about this night and day for six months, Abby. Watching you and thinking about how you seem to hate everything I ever touched, including the food I've been putting on your table for eighteen years. It ain't easy — no, it ain't been easy being reviled and threatened that way day in, day out." He rolls down his window and throws his cigarette out.

"Don't do that, Forrest. You'll start a fire on those dry leaves."

He curves over the steering wheel, white-knuckling it with both hands like he's riding a Harley. He doesn't look at her. "You may not believe me, but I love you, Abby." He stares out the windshield like he's watching for something. "I do love you but I can't live this way, waiting." He smooths his hair, the curls go flat, then spring up as his huge hand passes over his head. "I'm ready for you to leave now. The children and I will be just fine — you saw how I cooked dinner tonight, and the kids cleaned up and you ain't been home to get them off in the morning for months."

It is a clear night. A few stars are out and Abby can see the sharp outline of Forrest's face in the starlight. She thinks of the first time she saw him, playing football, at night. He stood just below her seat in the stands and took off his helmet and pushed his hair back. He was breathing heavy then, too, and in the car, now, in the dark, he looks just as fine as he did then. "What exactly are you saying, Forrest?" She puts her cigarette out in the ashtray.

"I just want to know when this is all going to be over. Seems like it's some kind of game for you, but it's been hell for me." His big shoulders heave — like he's out of breath or crying. "I've been waiting for the other shoe to drop for too long. I can't stand this no more. Are you going or staying?" He raises his head and his face shines in the starlight.

"Well, I don't exactly know," she begins.

His big hand slams on the steering wheel. "You been doing me this way for too long. Quit playing with me. You think I'm some kind of joke, some monster with no feelings, you can just taunt me and walk all over me and think you got some new, great life. Well, it is over now. I ain't taking any more. You tell me now — you staying or you going? And if you're going then we pack up your things this weekend and that's it."

"It's not that easy, Forrest. What about the children? Where will I go?"

"The children will stay at home where they belong."

"I can't lose the kids and Willie, too."

"Damn it, Abby, Willie is grown up and getting along fine. You seen the picture he sent."

She starts to shake. "You can't take the kids," she says.

"I ain't taking, Abby," Forrest says. "If you'll notice, it's you who's leaving. The kids and I aren't going anywhere."

"But where will I go?" she says. "I don't think you can just throw me out like this, Forrest. It's not right."

"They got apartment buildings right across from your mall. You get an apartment there and I'll even give you the first month's rent. After that, your boyfriend Jake can help you."

At the mention of Jake, Abby starts to cry. "He's not my boyfriend."

"You talk about him enough."

She puts her hand on his arm. It is as hard as an oak tree. "You said you loved me. It sure don't feel like it."

He twists towards her, still gripping the steering wheel. "I can't talk about that any more. I can't come home to that house every night not knowing if I'll find you or what trash we going to eat or what dumb thing I'm going to do for you to make fun of. I don't know what killed our marriage but I can't live like this no more." He starts the car. "I guess we'll be one of those numbers in the newspapers — the split-up couple. If other folks can do it, so can I. I can't live with this in-between stuff."

*

FRIDAY morning is foggy and damp, heavy like after a hard rain. The trees and bushes look swept clean and ready to burst into leaf.

The peach and plum trees Forrest planted around the house are dotted with green buds. Abby brushes against pale, feathery pine needles as she walks to the bus stop. The new needles are as soft as baby's hair.

She had asked Forrest if he wanted her to sleep on the couch and he had said no, so they lay back to back, the two of them silent and awake, not touching, trying to stifle their breathing. She had told him she would leave and she lay with her mind blank, trying to know what she meant. Willie's face faded in and out. She saw him washing dishes and playing with the cat and once he said, "Mom" but when she reached out, it was black again and all she heard was Forrest's heavy breathing. She got up first and left for work while he was still in the bathroom.

She sits in the back of the bus and leans her head on the damp glass. Her arms are heavy in her lap and she dozes until a boy in a jeans jacket and white Reeboks sits down beside her. He is listening to a radio, earphones in his ears, slightly moving to the buzz she hears from his radio. Willie used to do that, she thinks. Willie's like this boy, only bigger. The boy shaves and looks like he can take care of himself. "I needed space too, like Willie," she says and the boy turns to her, expectantly.

When she gets off at the mall, she stands and stares at the high rise across the street — Clintock Condominiums. They probably all have dishwashers, she thinks. A huge red banner that says NOW RENTING in yellow letters dangles from the roof. In the fog the building reminds her of a mountain peak, the Smokies shrouded in mist when they drove down from Gatlinburg. She gets the queasy feeling she had on those narrow roads when she looks at Clintock Condominiums. Then she turns and walks across the mall parking lot to the employees' entrance.

She's late. She pushes up the bars to the store and scoots under and opens a drawer to put her purse away. It is warm and close. She reaches to flip on the lights and someone puts his hand on her arm and pulls her off balance. She yelps and Jake puts his soft palm over her mouth. "Shhhh, baby," he says. "It's just me, waiting for you. Why are you so late? I thought you'd come early today." His hand smells like the lilac aftershave they import from England.

"Oh," she says, laughing, and then she starts to sob, tears running down her face and over his hand. He holds her gently and guides her into the store room. She can't stop crying and she can't say anything to him. He pulls her down on the futon. "I love it when a woman is emotional," he says. "I can't wait either, honey."

She shakes her head, crying, "No," she says, "no." He has unbuttoned her blouse and is fumbling for her bra hook. "No," she says again. "Oh, please, no." She pushes him away but he laughs and pins her hands beside her head and kisses her hard on the mouth.

"This will be even better than yesterday, because now we are experienced with each other," he says. "The second time is always better."

She sits up suddenly and hits his nose with the crown of her head. He loses his balance and falls down beside her, rubbing his face. "Hey, Honey, it's all right."

"No, it's not all right." She finds the hook of her bra. "You do this all the time, don't you?"

He smiles and kisses her neck. "Don't talk so much, sweetheart," he says. "You are with a master. Your old man doesn't know the art of loving like I do."

She feels his teeth on her ear and she hits the side of his face as hard as she can. "I quit," she screams. "I quit. I quit everything. Don't touch me." She clutches her blouse and jumps up, fumbling with the buttons.

"What in the hell is eating you?" he says.

"Don't you move. Just stay there." He stays cross-legged on the futon, a half-smile visible through his beard, as she backs away.

"You got me wrong, Abigail. I like you," he says.

She runs to the front of the store, buttoning her blouse. The catch on the cage has caught and she struggles to release it so she can get out. A man with a cane walks by with his arm around a white-haired lady wearing running shoes. They stop and smile at her. "Need help, Miss?" the man asks.

Abby laces her fingers through the wires of the cage and jiggles it enough to release the lock. "No," she says. "I'm a little stuck, but I'll figure it out." The couple walk on. She lifts the cage over her head and slips out.

Facing Mount Kenya

THE MOUNTAIN HASN'T FORGOTTEN US. I still come to the veranda at dawn to watch its gentle exhalation of cloud and sky. Jane irons there during the day and at night Joseph and I take our coffee out to the wicker chairs. We seldom mention our daughter Wanjiro, but on the veranda, I can smell her damp, flowered breath and see her translucent skin the color of walnuts and feel her hand on my arm and breast, a sweet, soft spider finding its way. I know she would have changed, developed bumps and nicks like the rest of us if she had lived, I know that, but when I sit facing Mount Kenya, I remember her staring at me with eyes black as a collapsed star and that empty place in my stomach widens and she is a part of me again.

She was a part of Joseph, too, of course. He has the same liquid eyes, like drops of oil, and skin so black that his beard doesn't show.

The day we met, at the University International Fair '66, he stared at me for twenty minutes as I pushed a clump of ugali around the edge of my plate, trying to figure out how to eat it. Finally, I scraped my fingers on the plate and said, "This stuff has the consistency of day-old Cream of Wheat and tastes just as good."

He lifted his head and smiled. "Ugali is the staple food of my country. Very nutritious." He scooped up a bit with two fingers, neatly carrying meat and gravy, and placed it in his mouth. "You see, ugali is easy to eat."

When I dipped my fingers in the ugali again, he reached over and curved his hand around mine. "Gently, like this," he said and fed me a bite.

Then he leaned back as I ate and stared at me some more. He watched me for several minutes, not eating, not speaking or smiling when I made little jokes. He made me nervous.

"You look the way a woman should look," he said, at last. "You have the classic female shape."

I laughed and wiped my hand on my jeans under the table. "You mean the classic pear?" I said.

He looked puzzled and smiled. "I like the way you look," he said. "You are quite beautiful." I would have followed him to Timbuktu to hear that again.

It was easy to love him, a gentle man, bland but satisfying, like his cuisine, and the fact that my marrying a foreigner and a black man made my mother madder than hell was in his favor. I don't know why she even cared because she never expected me to get married at all, but she kept asking me how I could do this to her, how could I do this to her? When I said do what? she yelled louder and said don't be smart. When I pointed out that we would be going to Kenya as soon as Joseph finished his degree, she calmed down. Her friends wouldn't see us and she wouldn't see us but she would still have this mildly interesting daughter. She gave us luggage as a wedding present and we left Minnesota right after graduation.

*

JOSEPH wrote his thesis on coffee cultivation, and got a job managing a coffee scheme, a cooperative where farmers divide the work and share the profits. It was very experimental and everybody was anxious that it succeed, so he spent a lot of time driving ministry big shots around the scheme. He was disgusted at first and said he didn't spend five years at the university to chauffeur carloads of government officials, but as he became politically more sensitive, he said the visiting Wabenzi were the guys who paid for the lost screws when the cultivator fell apart. It was his job to educate them.

My job was managing the household. I told Joseph I didn't want any servants, that it was demeaning work, but Musa, the old man who takes care of the yard, was a fixture of the house and Kamau, our first cook, came to us through Joseph's extended family.

Kamau and his wife Jane showed up the day after we arrived, carrying bundles on their heads. I was unpacking wedding presents in the kitchen and didn't hear them come in. I straightened up to lift a stack of plates to the shelf and there they both were, standing in my shadow, not three feet away. I nearly dropped the dishes.

"Joseph," I called, "come quickly."

"Meet your cook," Joseph said when he came in. "This is Kamau and his wife."

Jane and Kamau smiled broadly and bowed to me.

I couldn't believe it. "I have a degree in Home Ec," I said. "We don't need a cook."

Joseph wasn't listening.

"We can't afford servants," I protested.

Kamau and Joseph were speaking rapid Kikuyu together and laughing like brothers. Jane and I stared at each other, with tight little smiles on our faces. I learned later that she was Maragoli, from the far west, and didn't understand much more Kikuyu than I did. When they left to inspect their new quarters, Joseph turned to me. "You'll like Kamau," he said. "He is a good man."

"It's not a question of liking," I said. "I don't want a cook. It's ridiculous for the two of us to have a cook and a yard man."

"A man in my position must have servants. It's expected. In America, I kept silent and learned your ways. Now you must learn."

"But servants, Joseph? It's so un-American."

He laughed and took my hand. "Kamau is of my age group — we were initiated together. We will help him. It is not a matter of choice." As it turned out, many things were not a matter of choice — my husband's monthly salary contributed to the school fees of several brothers or cousins and our garden was freely harvested by his family.

The in-law situation was overwhelming for me, an only child. There is no Kikuyu word for uncle or aunt so Joseph had six fathers and the mamas were even more numerous — small, wiry women who smelled like butter when they hugged me. My mother didn't believe in touching. She thought any display of affection made you weak so she never came near me except to drag a comb through my hair or to flick a stray something off my collar. She used those occasions to remind me that I was just like my father. I don't remember him but I have his high school football picture that I used to keep in my dresser drawer. He is crouched down, one arm planted in the grass, the other on his knee. He has on his helmet so you can't see much about his face; but if he were just like me, he had hardly any eyebrows and pale eyelashes and freckles and probably zits everywhere. You can tell that he was big and broad, too. I'm not as tall, thank goodness, but I've got shoulders like a wrestler. Joseph saw the picture when we were unpacking and the next time he went to Nairobi, he bought me a frame for it and now it hangs in the sitting room of our house.

Joseph's position provided us with an old stone house that was a relic of colonial days. It was eight kilometers up a dirt path off the main road north of Nyeri in the foothills below Mount Kenya. The house was elegant once and came furnished with Oriental rugs, oversized armchairs with ottomans, and a twelve-foot dining room table made of mahogany planks. The entire west wall of the sitting room is constructed of French doors hinged together and made to accordion open onto a large, roofed veranda. From the high veranda, the yard stretches four hundred feet. A tier of poinsettia trees below the house separates the kitchen garden from the wild, grassy area that slopes to a creek. Musa's goats graze there — he was going to give a kid to Wanjiro as soon as she could walk. A scraggly mulberry tree droops at the corner of the garden. The tightly woven nests of the weaver birds dangle from its branches like so many silk purses. The weaver birds are bold and chatty and come right up to the veranda for the seeds Jane sprinkles along the railing.

But it's the mountain that dominates the house. We sit on the veranda and watch it or, rather, watch for it because most of the time Mount Kenya is hidden in clouds. The peaks are usually visible only in the early morning. When I was nursing Wanjiro I would take her out on the veranda and sit, facing the mountain. Often we were there before dawn, and just as the sun came up, we would see the snowcap shining like a great light. The Kikuyu call it Kere-Nyaga, mountain of brightness or mystery, the earthly resting place for Ngai. Sitting in that old rataan chair, with my baby at my breast pushing with her tiny hands, and pulling with her sweet mouth, watching the mystery mountain rise out of the darkness and mist with the sun as its halo was like seeing Ngai with my own eyes. I felt him in the cool morning air that moved slowly over my body. By seven o'clock when Jane came up to fix breakfast and Joseph was brushing his teeth in the bathroom, the mountain would be shrouded in clouds for the day, a sign that ordinary living could commence.

South of the house is a long, low frame building with rooms for servants — Musa, Kamau and Jane lived there. I seldom saw Musa but Kamau was a talented cook and I let him show me his stuff. I also taught him a few things and we got along well in the kitchen. My only problem with him was that he ironed all the towels every week and Joseph's jockey shorts. He loved to iron and I couldn't get him to stop on the towels. He pressed the fluff right out of them. Jane didn't work for us, at least not until later, after Kamau died. I didn't want her then, but I couldn't make her leave, and later, of course, I don't know what I would have done without her.

Kamau and Jane were about our age, mid-twenties, and I confess I never thought about their marriage or if they got along until one day Kamau appeared at the kitchen door on a Sunday, his day off, with a young Kikuyu girl.

"This my wife," he said, in English. "Margaret."

Margaret was young and shy — she didn't raise her eyes above my belt buckle. I looked at her in astonishment.

"What about Jane?" I asked.

"Oh, she gone," Kamau said. "I send her back to her father." He looked at Margaret fondly. "I must have children. Jane no give me sons."

So I shook Margaret's hand and called Joseph in to meet her.

Later I said to Joseph, only half in jest, "Well, is that what you Kikuyu do when your wife doesn't produce children, send them back to their father?" I'd boiled water for tea and I handed him a cup. "You know, we don't really know where my father is, so it might be a problem."

He smiled and said, "That is the old way and he would not have done that if she were Kikuyu. The old women have made him superstitious about marrying outside the tribe."

"Have you forgotten that I'm not Kikuyu either?"

"You never told me that." He laughed and put his arm around me and kissed my cheek. "I would like a son, if you can arrange it," he said.

I promised to try and I forgot about Jane and her exile until the day Tom Mboya was shot outside a Nairobi drugstore. We were having tea with Roland Kinyabe, the school headmaster, at the Outspan in Nyeri when the news came.

"What luck, Joseph," said Roland. "Mboya killed in a robbery."

Joseph looked at him sharply. "He was assassinated," he said. He wiped his mouth with his hand and looked away. "It sounds like he was murdered by one of us."

Roland smiled and shook his head. "We must be realistic, my friend," he began.

Joseph stood up quickly. "Is this why we fought for independence, to murder our own Kenyan people?"

"Don't get excited, Joseph," Roland said. "You know Mboya was too popular."

Joseph turned to me. "Put your cup down. We are leaving."

"But I haven't finished my tea," I said.

"Forget the tea," he said. "We are going home."

He clamped his hand on my elbow and helped me up — I was six months pregnant at the time. I felt like I'd been taken hostage as he steered me around the plush chairs and polished tables to the door. Roland called after us but Joseph pretended not to hear.

In the car, I said, "You were rude to Roland and inconsiderate of me. I wasn't ready to leave."

Joseph didn't even look at me. We drove home in silence.

The house was dark when we turned in. I remember saying, "I wonder where Kamau is. He should be cooking dinner." We got out of the car and it was unusually still: no Kikuyu children waiting for a candy, no mamas passing with water jugs, not even the scratch and cackle of chickens from the village below. The only sound was the generator pumping away. I walked through to the kitchen, turned on a light, and there he was, kneeling on the floor, bent over as if he were trying to hold himself together until we got home. His head was resting in bread dough, indented like a down pillow, the dough rising over and around his face, the blood pooled under his body. Kamau must have been kneading bread when they came for him. It took me a minute to realize that he was dead and then I started screaming.

It was Musa's day off and Margaret was nowhere to be found and we had no phone. We got back in the Land Rover and drove to Nyeri for the police, stopping only once for Joseph to inform Kamau's people. Their compound was a ten-minute walk up a footpath that branched off from the dirt road and I waited in the car, but I knew when Joseph reached them. The women's voices rose high and sharp and their wailing resounded in my ears for days.

When the business with the police was done, I wanted to stay in town. I didn't want to go home to my kitchen and secluded house, but Joseph refused. At first I thought he was like my mother, disdainful of my fears, but later I realized it was Mboya he was thinking of. He didn't want to spend the night in a public place in the middle of Kikuyu country and participate in the celebration of the death of a gifted Luo politician. It was odd; the murders seemed exactly the same to me, two men killed because they were of the wrong tribe, but Joseph was sickened by Mboya's death and not by Kamau's, which occurred in front of his own kitchen sink. He seemed to feel that Kamau's death was inevitable, or at least predictable. "It was Jane's family," was all he said. That's the way it is here — you feel that death is close, a part of life. Kamau always prayed over a chicken before he killed it, but he killed it. "Praise ye, Ngai," they sang at his funeral. "Peace be with us."

I began then to see my husband as a divided man, twice educated — his public behavior following the course of western thought while his private life conformed instinctively to tribal ways. That's why I can't blame him for what happened later, for saying no when he should have said yes.

*

MARGARET went back to her family. I was sitting on the veranda a week later, feeling my baby kick and shift in my womb and staring at the mountain, when Jane appeared at the side of the house. I was startled by her appearance. She looked dusty and gaunt, as if she had been walking ever since Kamau threw her out. She dropped her bundle at the edge of the garden, picked up a bucket, and walked down the hill towards the creek, disappearing from sight as she passed through the poinsettias. Joseph had already left for work so I was alone except for Musa. I ran to the old man's room and knocked on the door as hard as I could. I heard him shuffle across the dirt floor, and he opened the door only a crack. He jumped to attention when he saw me, catching himself just short of a salute. I would have laughed if I weren't so scared.

"Jane is here," I said, urgently.

He stood ramrod straight and looked at me politely, waiting.

"She is here, she's come back," I said. "You know, Jane, Kamau's first wife, the one who had him killed."

He nodded at me slowly, like a deaf person, or like somebody who is being patient with a very young child. I was beginning to feel foolish.

"Well, what do you suppose she is going to do, Musa?" I said.

He looked at me a moment longer, then spoke, "She is home, Memsahib. She have no other place."

"But, her father?" I began, but the old man shook his head.

"No," he said, "this is the only place she have. I have waited for her." He bowed to me again and closed his door. I heard him shuffle back to his bed.

When I turned around, she was standing at the corner of the little building, washing her arms and face. I took a step towards her and spoke as sharply as I could. "What are you doing here, Jane?" I said. "I ought to call the police."

She shook her head and continued rinsing her face and arms. "No," she said. "I here to help you."

I backed away. Jane was as heavy as I was and several inches taller. "It didn't help me, killing Kamau," I said.

"I was good wife." She turned to me. She didn't have a towel and the water ran down her face like tears. "Kamau shame me. Send me back. I do nothing. It is my brothers' business." She picked up her bundle. "I come home," she said.

I didn't know what to do, so I went in the house and locked all the doors.

Jane waited in the garden, framed by the mountain rising in the mist behind her. She stared at the house all day. I didn't want to face her, but by three o'clock, I couldn't stand it any longer so I left by the front door and walked quietly around the house to spy on her. For some reason I thought that she would advance on the house as soon as it was empty. But she still stood among the rows of beans. Finally, I realized that I had been waiting for Jane to do something, but she was not the one with power. I was the Memsahib.

It was hot and the sun had burned off most of the mist that usually clouds the top of Mt. Kenya. I could almost see the outline of the peaks through the vapour. So I made one of those bargains with myself that people make when they don't know what to do, but they don't want responsibility for the decision. "If the clouds clear completely and I can see Mt. Kenya, I will let Jane in to work for us," I said. It would be a sign from Ngai, I thought. I waited for a long time, sweaty and tired, and was ready to send Jane away when a cloud passed overhead, offering momentary relief from the heat. I looked toward the mountain; it was clear and the snowcap was visible – a sign from Ngai. I smiled to myself at the success of my plan and walked back around the house, in the front door, and through to the back to open the kitchen door. I stood on the steps and looked at Jane but I didn't say anything. She came slowly and stiffly climbed the stairs.

"Are ugali and beef good tonight?" was all she said.

"Yes, Jane," I said, "that will be fine." I left her in the kitchen and went to lie down until Joseph came home.

*

AFTER that Jane took over Kamau's duties. She had not cooked European food before, and after the third day of ugali and boiled meat, I began teaching her new recipes. We liked each other. She was a shade lighter than the Kikuyu and had the roundest, most sensuous lips I have ever seen on a woman. She only had one dress when she came and, since we wore the same size, I began to give her a few things I didn't need. She refused any trousers but she wept when I gave her an old nightgown with a matching robe. "Thank you, Memsahib," she said. "I never have sleeping clothes."

I liked having another woman about the house. I felt less obligated to get completely dressed in the morning; I could wander through the living room in my slip, or sit on the veranda in my robe; I didn't feel so shy about grabbing a couple of cookies when I walked through the kitchen. With Kamau I always felt I had some sort of formal role to act out. With Jane, I was able to be myself, and gradually that old colonialist house begin to feel like my house and the days felt like my days. I liked it there. Jane taught me a little Swahili, I taught her a little English. I showed her how to use my sewing machine; she showed me how to cut open the immature papaya and use it as a salve for burns or bites.

Mary Wanjiro Calhoun Nduta was born three months later, September 19, 1969. The details of the labor are lost to me but I remember Dr. Bashal saying, "It's a girl." I raised up before the cord was cut and my daughter stared right at me, glistening like an otter; and when they laid her on my belly, I could feel her swimming towards me. I pulled her to my breast and she found my nipple and held on. As her mouth smacked against my skin, I felt really connected to another human being for the first time in my life.

On the morning I returned from the hospital, Jane was standing at the end of the drive when we drove up. She followed the Land Rover as we turned in, keeping her hand on the fender, then stood under the bougainvillea that spreads across the corner of the house to watch as Joseph helped me out of the car. I walked over to her. "Do you want to see Mary Wanjiro?" I asked.

She smiled with her beautiful lips and said, "Yes, Memsahib, I wait a long time." She bent over my baby and took one of the tiny hands in hers and sang a little welcome song. Then I asked if she wanted to hold the baby and she took Wanjiro from me so tenderly that we both started to cry and laugh together. I felt at that moment that Jane was the only woman who ever understood me. Then Musa came to see the baby, and Joseph took Wanjiro and rocked her. I was to learn in those first days that a child is valued above all things in that country, by men and women alike. When we took Wanjiro to the coffee scheme, all the men came running to see her and to exclaim over her and to hold her. I couldn't help but wonder what would happen if I had taken her to my mother's office. I couldn't imagine my mother holding a baby, and certainly the other brokers wouldn't swarm around to get their turn to have her in their arms. Joseph never said another word about a son.

*

WANJIRO and the mountain were the first things I saw every morning. I spread a rug on the veranda and she spent her day there, with me or Jane looking on. While she nursed, I told her stories about the first Wanjiro, daughter of the man Giguyu, founder of her people, who viewed their land from the peaks of Mount Kenya; and my other stories all had a brave girl named Wanjiro who lived on a great mountain.

By the time she was two months old, Joseph held her on his lap during dinner every night, feeding her from his plate.

"Dr. Spock says she shouldn't have solid food yet," I said, but he just smiled patiently at me.

"You forget she is half Kikuyu," he said, speaking as if he were lecturing his men. "My daughter can eat anything."

I didn't argue, but I was prepared to shake her by the heels and pound her back when she gagged on the bits of rice he put in her mouth.

At five months, she talked to herself continually as she sat on the veranda, waving her arms at the weaver birds. If the birds squabbled over a seed, she would shout and pull herself up on her hands and knees and bounce and look around, lifting one arm to move forward, threatening to crawl, and then she'd fall on her belly and pull herself to the edge of the rug. Jane and I laughed at her, challenging the birds. Warrior Wanjiro, I called her. She was a big, healthy girl, twice the size of the Kikuyu babies in the village.

Joseph invented games for her at about that time. "Look how strong she is," he said to me one day as he held her in front of him, standing up, with her two little feet in his hand.

"Oh, Joseph, don't do that." I was alarmed to see her wavering, unsupported on his hand. "How can she hold herself up? I'm sure it's bad for her."

Wanjiro laughed, pleased with herself.

"Watch this," Joseph said and put one hand under her stomach and the other on her legs and propelled her, undulating, through the air like an airplane. Joseph and Wanjiro had the same delighted grin on their faces.

"Joseph, stop it. You might hurt her." I wanted to enjoy their fun, but the games made me uneasy.

One morning I woke up earlier than usual and got up to check on her. She was very still under the mosquito netting so I lit a candle — the generator wouldn't crank on for another hour or so. Wanjiro looked as if she had shrunk in the night. She was awake and her liquid black eyes stared at me but she didn't move or smile. "Oh, baby," I said, the fear rising in my body. I set down the candle, raised the netting, and leaned in to pick her up. Her body radiated the sharp heat of an animal that has lain all day in the sun. She started to whimper immediately, as if I were hurting her just by touching her. I laid her down carefully and ran to grind up baby aspirin, then mixed it with honey and offered it to her on a spoon. She turned her head away, so I picked her up and took her out to the veranda. Again I offered her the aspirin, but her little bow mouth wouldn't open. I twisted and pushed the spoon to force it through her lips, but she wouldn't swallow. The honey oozed around her mouth, sticky like sap covering a wound on a tree. I dabbed frantically at the pink grains of aspirin caught in the honey sliding down her chin. "Please, please, take this, Wanjiro," I said.

It was just dawn and I couldn't see the mountain. It wouldn't clear that day. Dr. Spock said to give the baby a cool bath for the fever, so I woke Joseph to help me.

"It's malaria," he said when he saw her. "She must have a terrible headache, too, but it will pass." He put his arm around me and kissed the top of my head. "Our poor girl," he said. "She'll be all right."

He helped me with the bath and, as her temperature slowly dropped, she became less listless. At a hundred and one she took the syrup and baby aspirin. Joseph insisted on giving her a little chloroquine, even though I was afraid to, since we didn't know for sure if she did have malaria or the proper dosage for a baby.

"Let's take her to Nyeri, Joseph, to the doctor. I've never seen her like this." I put my head on his shoulder and he held me for a minute without speaking.

"Don't worry, my dear," he said, gently rubbing my back. "I know malaria. See, she is better already. Just keep her cool and let her rest and she will be fine when the fever breaks."

I had never seen anybody with malaria and she didn't seem to be shaking and chattering the way I had imagined malaria victims. But she was listless and hot and cried when I picked her up. "I still think we should take her in."

"She is a strong baby," he said, "and she'll be better in a few days. We don't run to the doctor for ordinary illnesses here." He left us sitting on the veranda and went to work.

When Jane came, she looked at Wanjiro and shook her head, clicking her tongue sadly against her teeth.

"Bwana says it is malaria, Jane. What do you think?"

She picked up Wanjiro and laid her cheek on the baby's cheek and then looked carefully at her eyes. "Yes, is malaria," she said.

"She is much better now," I said. "You should have seen her this morning."

Jane shook her head and laid Wanjiro back in my arms. "Will be bad again tomorrow," she said without smiling.

When Joseph came home I begged him again to take us to the doctor. I told him what Jane had said, and he shook his head patiently. "Believe me, my dear, I know. This will only last a day or two more and then she will be perfect."

But she wasn't perfect. She lay listless in my arms the next day. I took her onto the veranda because it was cool out there and I came to believe that the fresh air and the protection of the mountain were essential to her recovery. I began to promise Ngai a number of things if he would just help Wanjiro.

I thought she was failing steadily but still Joseph wouldn't take us to the doctor. I was powerless before his calm reassurances and tried repeatedly to tell him of my fears. I begged him for my sake, if not for hers, to let us go into Nyeri. He refused. I began to hate him. I didn't understand why we couldn't make a simple trip to the doctor. "I want to take her home, to Minnesota," I said on the third day. "We can take her to the Mayo Clinic."

He looked at me sharply. "You must learn to live in this country." He said there was trouble on the scheme with one of the machines and he left.

I stood alone and afraid on the front porch, holding Wanjiro and hating my husband.

Jane was waiting when I went back in the house. She had been in the kitchen, listening to us argue. "What can we do?" I said, crying as I looked at my baby, listless and pale.

"We will take her to Nyeri."

"But he took the car . . ." I began.

"Don't worry," she said. "Somebody will give us ride." She put her hands on her hips and stood beautiful as a sculpture, gazing at Wanjiro, her lovely lower lip protruding and the sad tongue clicks coming from her mouth. She was silhouetted against the rising mist.

The mountain was still shrouded but the clouds seemed higher.

"I think we will see the mountain today," I said.

She nodded and smiled. "If we see the mountain, it is a sign Wanjiro will be well." She bent over and kissed Wanjiro swiftly on both cheeks. "We go soon," she said. "I get ready."

I laid the baby in her crib. Her eyes fluttered continually and I couldn't tell if she were awake or asleep. I pulled on tennis shoes and a loose cotton dress that I had worn when I was pregnant. It would be a long, hot day.

When Jane returned, she said, "I will carry Wanjiro."

"She is too sick to be on your back," I said.

"Don't worry, Memsahib. I know how to carry her." Jane doubled a long strip of cloth and lay Wanjiro in it. Even though she was seven months old, she had lost weight and lay limp as a newborn. When Jane hefted her up, she didn't resist. Jane tied the cloth around her own back and neck and Wanjiro hung suspended in front, hammock-like. I put a baby bottle and a couple of mangoes in a bag and we were ready by seven-thirty. I thought of leaving Joseph a note, but our departure felt like an escape and I couldn't bring myself to tell him where we were going. I was afraid he would come after us and bring us back. He could easily catch up with us if we didn't get a ride by lunchtime when he came home.

It was a cool, humid morning. The sun was still low in the sky and the light filtering through the moisture in the air gave a dreamlike quality to the day. When I think of that day now it always has the look and feel of a dream: muted colors, slow moving bodies, faces of strangers emerging briefly in the mist to speak to us and then fading back into the fog. We had to walk eight kilometers to reach the tarmac. We would have no chance of a ride until then. I thought of all the times we had passed people walking along that road, people who had waved us down. Joseph always stopped and the first time I had said, "Do you think it is safe to pick up hitchhikers?"

He had laughed and said, "These are just poor people who need a ride. Nobody is dangerous here. It is my car, but everybody feels I must give him a ride if he needs it. They would do the same for me."

I remembered that and felt hopeful. We would get to Nyeri.

Jane was as heavy as I was, yet I could hardly keep up with her.

I had to take quick little steps every twenty seconds or so and soon I was panting. But I didn't say a word because we had to get to Nyeri. Wanjiro hadn't moved or whimpered since we started. Jane kept one arm under her and she lay, slightly turned towards Jane's body, still and small. I tried to talk to her as we hurried along. "It's going to be okay, Baby," I'd say. "Jane and your mama are taking you to the doctor. We'll get you well." And then I couldn't talk for a while and would just concentrate on walking. The road was rutted and uneven and continually curved back on itself; our view switched from the plains ending in forest to the mountain rising into the clouds. Everytime we faced Kere-Nyaga, I evaluated the height of the clouds. We hadn't seen the peak since Wanjiro took sick. It seemed important that we see the mountain soon.

We were not alone on our trek. A woman with a small boy on her hip joined us almost immediately and walked with us for a few minutes and then started to talk to Jane in Swahili. Because of Jane's notoriety among the Kikuyu women, I was curious to know what they talked about. My Swahili was spotty, but as far as I could tell, the conversation was mundane — where are you going, who is the memsahib, what is wrong with the baby. The woman pulled back the cloth around Wanjiro and made that sad clicking noise with her tongue. I was to hear that sound all morning as people looked at my baby. They all did it, men, women, children, and shook their heads. You would think that it would get on my nerves, this incessant clicking, but it brought a lump to my throat for my sick baby. I had felt alone all my life until Wanjiro came and now, in my hour of desperation, these people walked with me, extending their hearts with indrawn breath and clicks of the tongue. One woman kissed me before leaving us for a narrower path.

The road passed through a mountain stream. Jane took off her plastic shoes. "Is better, Memsahib," she said. As a fat girl growing up in Minneapolis, I never went barefoot, never played in the creek, because I was afraid of slipping or exposing myself in some unforeseen manner. I held my shoes and skirt in one hand and started cautiously across, my free arm waving to maintain my balance. An old grandmother caught my soft hand in her tiny hard one and led me across, saying, "Mzuri, Mzuri, Mzuri." She patted me on the back when I safely reached the other side. I was embarrassed and put my hand on Wanjiro's cheek.

"Jane, let's bathe Wanjiro, to cool her. She is too warm again."
We sat under a huge chestnut tree and the children ran back and
forth to the stream, soaking cloths. Wanjiro lay on my lap, and we
stroked her thin arms and legs with the cool cloths and washed her
face and head. Her eyes fluttered open and she looked right at me,
I'm sure. She tried to smile but she was so weak and tired. Her lips
trembled, trying to open. I looked towards the mountain. The
clouds were rising.

By the time we reached the main road, most of our companions
had dropped away and the few who remained turned in the opposite
direction, on their way to the Friday market. Jane and I walked
alone along the tarmac. I was carrying Wanjiro now, slung around
my back and neck like Jane. I couldn't keep up with Jane's pace, but
I needed to carry her myself. Jane knew that without my explaining
and had nodded and smiled when I asked her for the baby. I'm not
strong and have this weight problem, and my heart was pumping
hard the whole time, but the worse part was that Wanjiro was easy
to carry. Like carrying a doll or a kitten. The cloth was hot on my
neck and my arm under her got tired but she seemed shrunken and
weightless, a butterfly baby that we carried along the Nyeri Road.

We walked for thirty minutes and no vehicle passed us. "Don't
worry, Memsahib," Jane said. "The first one will stop."

The safari bus never slowed down. Jane and I bent towards the
trees as one person, shielding ourselves and the baby from the dust.
"I didn't even get my hand up," I said.

"Is all right," she said. "Those zebra cars don't stop. We waiting
for a person by himself."

The mountain is never out of sight on the Nyeri Road. Even when
we walked down in a hollow we could see it rising to our left. I
thought of the lodge at Nanyuki where Joseph and I had met a party
of climbers, men with axes and crampons who were leaving the
next morning to go up. They were excited and said it was the best
climbing in Africa, even better than Kilimanjaro, because of the
challenge of Batian, the high peak. Joseph had been upset by the
conversation and later told me that he thought the government
should keep people like that out of the country. I thought he was
being silly. He knew as well as anybody that the tourist dollar is the
number one source of foreign revenue, and at least they weren't
shooting elephants. "Kere-Nyaga is more important than any

elephant," he had said. I remember thinking that here was something else I would never understand. But walking that day under the protection of the mountain, I felt that it was sacred, a holy place, and if a man ascends the mystery peaks and takes pictures then the resting place of Ngai is violated. How can Ngai return to a place hacked by axes and despoiled by pitons hammered into rock? There must be some place for God alone.

*

WE heard the Land Rover before we saw it, laboring up the hill, and Jane stationed herself across the road to flag it down. The car veered around her and stopped on the shoulder ahead. A white man in khaki shorts and shirt got out and walked back to us. "Your girl could get killed standing in the road like that," he shouted. He was Australian. "You got a problem?"

I was out of breath when I reached him and could hardly speak. I pulled back the cloth to show him Wanjiro. "My baby is very sick," I said. "Could you give us a lift to Nyeri?"

He shook his head. "I'm going to Nairobi."

Jane had already opened the rear door of the Rover. "Okay," I said. "That's even better. We will go to the doctor in Nairobi."

"Lady, that's a hundred and fifty kilometers." He turned to walk back to his car.

I hurried after him, my heart pounding, Wanjiro swinging from me in her hammock. "Then drop us at Nyeri — it's only a little out of your way, and my baby is dying."

"Twenty kilometers out of my way," he said. "What are you doing out here with a native baby, anyhow?"

"Get in the car, Jane," I said. She was already in. I handed Wanjiro to her and crawled in the back myself. The man just watched us, not moving. I pulled the door closed, and he still stood there. Finally, he took off his cap, smoothed back his hair, walked to the driver's seat and got in.

"All right," he said. "I'll take you to Nyeri."

The ride was worse than the walking. The tarmac was pitted and Wanjiro bounced around on my lap. It was as if the force of gravity couldn't keep her. Jane and I took turns holding her in our arms, away from our bodies so we could protect her from the jarring ride.

She cried like a lost kitten, a soft, helpless wail, not as if she expected anybody to help her, but with cries forced out of her.

He dropped us in front of Dr. Bashal's office. "Allow me to pay you for your trouble," I said to him when we got out, fishing in my pockets for money. I did have money, after all, and he had made us feel like such beggars. But he waved me off and was gone before I had located a twenty-shilling note.

Dr. Bashal's office was filled with people. Jane, with Wanjiro, squeezed between two Indian women in saris on a narrow bench. A Kikuyu woman sat on a folding chair with two small boys in her lap, both with oozing sores on their legs. The man next to her slumped in a bent chair, asleep. Two men sat on the floor; three more stood against the wall. Everybody watched the door where the doctor would appear. Nobody spoke. The room was filled with the sighs and heavy breathing of the sick. Several people seemed as ill as Wanjiro, as if they, too, had waited until the last minute and then made a desperate effort to get to the doctor. I thought of Dr. Anderson's office at home — soft lighting, Muzak, and *The New Yorker*.

A young man in a blue shirt and blue work pants sat behind a white metal table in the middle of the room. He was writing in a large ledger.

"Do you have an appointment?" he said.

"No," I said. "My baby is terribly sick, we must see the doctor immediately."

He found a blank line with his finger. "Name?"

"Mary Wanjiro Nduta," I said. "It is malaria, we think."

He slowly printed her name in the ledger and wrote the number thirty-four next to it and wrote the number again on a square of white paper. He handed the paper to me. "This is your number. Can you come tomorrow at ten?"

I nearly burst into tears. "No," I said. "No. It is urgent. I must see the doctor today, now, right now." I banged my hand on his table and it wobbled dangerously. I clutched the table to steady it. "Look," I said, tears starting to form. "Look, see my child. Jane, bring Wanjiro here. Show him."

Jane came to the table and pulled back the cloth so the boy could see our baby. He looked at her and clicked his tongue against his teeth and shook his head. "Yes, I see. I will call you."

We waited a long time. There was nothing else to do. He called number twenty-two, and I thought I would die. A Kikuyu woman with a baby followed the boy through the low door. Her baby was smaller than Wanjiro and listless.

We were there an hour when Dr. Bashal himself came to the door to gaze about the waiting room. I hadn't seen him since he delivered Wanjiro. When he saw me on the bench, he spoke sharply to the boy at the white table, and the boy called number thirty-four next.

Dr. Bashal was one of those small, obsequious men with a pencil thin mustache and an ingratiating whine to his speech. "I am sorry you wait, Mrs. Nduta," he said. "If I had known you were here, I would see you immediately. Why didn't you tell my boy?"

"Please look at Wanjiro, Doctor," I said.

"Yes, of course," he said, and peeled back the cloth to look at her. He put his stethoscope on her thin chest, he gently felt her neck, examined her feet, looked carefully into her throat, took her temperature, weighed her, and then he shook his head.

"I am afraid that she is very sick, your baby," he said.

I could have felt sorry for him, he looked so apologetic, so helpless, but his words infuriated me. I knew she was sick. "What shall we do?"

"There is nothing to do. She has cerebral malaria." He washed his hands at the sink. "Perhaps if you had come sooner, but malaria, it is a bad thing and she has a rare case."

"Is there no medicine?" I said. "Can't you put her in the hospital?" I started to cry, to sob. I pleaded with him to give me hope, and he refused.

When I think of that day, it is all mist, except the twenty minutes in that little, white room. That is bright and clear and hard, a room with sharp edges and pure light from the bare bulb swinging overhead. There is no color, just white, and Jane's black face as she listened to him and his thin black hair and that black line of mustache under his nose. Even Wanjiro is white, deathly white, and the cloth that held her bleaches to lines and marks. He would do nothing.

We left. I remember leaning against the whitewashed building, sobbing and rocking Wanjiro, holding her to me, and when I looked up, I saw that the clouds were lower on the mountain. We stood on the street for several minutes. I couldn't face the trip home — begging for a ride, then walking the eight kilometers on the dirt road. I just couldn't do it. "We will stay here tonight, Jane," I said. "We will stay in a hotel." There was a little place down from the doctor's office. I knew Joseph would be upset for about a hundred reasons, not the least of which was that we went to this poor hotel. We should go to the famous Outspan to protect his position as an important man, but I couldn't face the mahogany paneling and the coffee on the veranda and the elegant buffet. I just wanted a room where nobody would notice me and my baby, and where Jane could stay with me. I didn't want to sleep alone with my baby in a beautiful room. So Jane and I got a room together and I asked her to go and find somebody who would take word to Joseph on the coffee scheme, who would tell him where we were. While she was gone, Wanjiro and I lay on the bed and I tried to nurse her; but she couldn't hold my breast in her mouth, she couldn't suck, not even from the bottle. So I tried to give her milk on a spoon but it dribbled down her chin and neck. I thought of the spring when I was eight years old and tried to feed a baby robin that had fallen from its nest in my back yard, a terrified baby bird, unable to swallow. It died the next day in the shoe box padded with cotton and scraps of terry cloth that I had made for it.

Joseph came before dawn to take us home. I drove so he could hold Wanjiro. He held her in his arms, away from his body, anticipating the jolts, trying to smooth her ride. "Did Bashal say we could give her aspirin and chloroquine?" he said.

"Yes."

"Nothing else will help?"

"No."

"But, it's too late?"

"Yes," I said. "Bashal says it's too late."

Wanjiro died two days later, in my lap, on the veranda. It was the day the clouds rose above the mountain. We were sitting there watching her and watching the clouds lift off the high peaks, the white spot of snow brilliant in the tropical sun and the morning mist blowing away and the clear light shining on us all. I heard the sound of a weaver bird taking a seed, then a sigh from Wanjiro. Her eyelids fluttered once, then her mouth sagged and I saw her two little teeth.

I pressed her to my breast and wept.

"Ngai take our baby home," Jane said and pulled her apron over her face.

Joseph laid his hand on her head. "Praise ye, Ngai," he said.

Disturbances

MRS. PICKENS STOOD AT THE DINING ROOM WINDOW, FROWNING at her scrubby yard and at the empty road beyond. She saw no trace of Okatch. So it's definite, she thought. He must be let go, a new watchman hired, and Willie's not around to do it.

She shuddered and picked a stiff, white hair off her bathrobe and held it between her thumb and forefinger. She was a small, spare woman who had expected to spend her life straightening pictures, fussing over drapery hems, and double-knotting her children's shoe laces before sending them off to school. But there were no pictures on her walls and the bare windows were shuttered from the outside and her child, Adelaide, had lived exactly one day. Mrs. Pickens often wondered if she could call herself a mother.

Willie took the post with the East African Railway the next year and she consoled herself with visions of bridge parties with the wives of diplomats, followed by high tea served on the large veranda of their colonial residence in the Kenyan highlands. But when Willie showed her the ugly little house they were to live in, she had wept. It was on the last street in Kisumu, on flat, treeless land that stretched unbroken for half a mile behind the house before rising sharply up the escarpment that marked the northern edge of the Rift

Valley. The three other houses on the road were occupied by Asians. Native huts were clumped across the plains behind the house and, if she opened her kitchen window, she could see spirals of smoke from their cooking fires and hear human voices. "Those people can walk right up to our back door," she had sobbed. "We don't even have a fence, much less a compound wall."

She had suffered in the house. She also had a rheumatic condition to be concerned with and a heart that beat faster than it should. Her voice carried a whispy undertone, and her breathing was punctuated with involuntary vocalizations that caused her husband to ignore her.

Well, she thought, he'll have to listen to me this time. She had pulled herself out of bed three times during the night to look for the beam from Okatch's flashlight. He had not been at his post by the front door nor had he been pacing the perimeter of the yard at the prescribed intervals. She despised Okatch and feared his predatory smile. Initiation scars lined his cheeks, and he had no teeth in his lower jaw. His primitive face gave her palpitations, and now she had cause for Willie to fire him. She wrapped the hair in a tissue and put it in her pocket, then eyed the road, patting her chest and taking deep breaths to calm her jittery heart.

A boy dragging a goat on a short lead appeared suddenly, right in front of her window, taking a short cut across her yard. She rapped on the glass to frighten him, but he ignored her. "I suppose this is what I'll have to endure until Willie comes home and gets me a new askari."

She sighed deeply, disturbing the layer of dust on the window. "Nobody notices the dirt here. Nobody cares but me," she said, dabbing at her eyes, then at the filthy glass, with her tissue.

The boy with the goat stopped on the road to talk to a man in a black overcoat. It was Okatch. She watched him bend toward the boy, then kneel to examine the goat. When he stood up, he shook the boy's hand. The boy said something that caused the animal to buck, Okatch jerked the lead, then the boy grabbed it, pulling the goat after him. The pair turned at the highway and disappeared. Okatch adjusted his coat and faced the house.

"Go away," Mrs. Pickens said to herself.

The watchman lifted his head as if he had heard her speak and started across the stubble.

She turned abruptly from the window and called to her girl. "Dorcas, I'll have my coffee now." She sat down, drumming the table with her brittle fingernails. She stopped almost immediately and pressed her hand into the wood. The sound of her tapping echoed in the room.

The girl, a Luo like Okatch, shuffled in with a plate of scrambled eggs and a cup of coffee. "Good morning, Memsahib," she said and hurried back to the kitchen, laughing.

"I only wanted coffee," Mrs. Pickens said. She tried to postpone breakfast by sipping coffee, but Dorcas refused to bring her food separately. I've never had decent help in this country, she thought, pushing the eggs away. She touched the cup to her lips, and tears filled her eyes. She couldn't eat another meal alone. She dropped the cup on the saucer without drinking and turned to the window.

"Oh, mercy!" she gasped and clutched her chest.

Okatch stood twelve inches away, on the other side of the screen. "Jambo, Mama," he said. "You are well?"

Mrs. Pickens thumped her chest with her fist and looked around for help. The kitchen door was closed. "Oh, no," she said. "Go! Finished!"

"How is Bwana Willie?" Okatch grinned and nodded at her.

"You are too late. We don't want you anymore."

He moved closer to the window.

Mrs. Pickens stood up and backed away. "You are fired, Okatch. No worki here no more." She flapped the back of her hand at him. "My husband pay you when he come."

Okatch shook his head, still smiling, and put his hand on the window. "Mama, I have big problem."

"Go away." She closed her eyes and clasped her hands together. "You are dismissed for unsatisfactory performance of your duties."

"You help me with motor car," he said, pointing to her Volkswagen and Willie's old Land Rover parked in the driveway.

Mrs. Pickens shook her head vehemently. She tried to crank the window closed, but he spread his hand across the glass. His fingernails were as yellowed and misshapen as an old man's.

"It is my sister's baby." He held the window. "Is too bad, but she dead yesterday."

She winced and rubbed her eyes to blur his face. "Your sister?"

Okatch shook his head. "Is her baby that dead," he said. "In hospital."

She couldn't move the window.

"No excuses, Okatch," she said. She didn't believe him for an instant. Willie told many stories of natives lying to cover their mistakes.

"You were expected here at six o'clock last night. I waited for you until dawn." She retied her bathrobe and smoothed her hair. "Because of you, I am not well rested."

He pointed in the direction of the provincial hospital. "We need take child home," he said. "The man on the bus not let us go with dead baby."

"You are finished, Okatch. Go away."

"We have no car."

"Mr. Pickens is not here and I can't help you," she said, clutching the windowsill. Her bones felt hollow and buoyant.

"Is not far to my father's house," Okatch said. "Twenty minutes on the road to Kakamega." He pressed the screen.

"Kindly move away from my window, or I shall call the police."

His body jerked as if he'd had the wind knocked out of him, and he dropped his hand and stepped back. She rolled the window closed, pulled the shade, and turned around, gasping and patting her chest.

Dorcas stood at the kitchen door, drying her hands on her apron. "You good, Memsahib?"

"That is an awful man, lying to me like that. I think he's intoxicated."

"He need your help," Dorcas said.

Mrs. Pickens held the back of a chair to steady herself. "He was hired to protect me. I cannot give him my car."

"He not ask you to give him car. He want you drive him."

Mrs. Pickens waved her arm at the girl and turned away. "There is no dead baby."

She took the newspaper into the sitting room, pulled the cord of the ceiling fan, and cautiously stretched out on the sofa. The sun crossed the room in flat sheets, making the air layered and visible. The warm air on her body was suffocating. She pressed her sharp knuckles against her eyebrows and closed her eyes. "I can't do it," she whispered. "I can't."

She floated between waking and sleeping and dreamed of her own dead child, Adelaide. It was too hot to sleep and she had the uneasy feeling that the sun was searing her eyelids, damaging the cornea while she lay there. She ought to get up. She pressed her fingers to her forehead and forced her eyes open. Dorcas stood at the end of the sofa.

"Oh, mercy, what do you want?"

"Memsahib, you must go to store," Dorcas said. "We have nothing to cook."

"Ah," she said, closing her eyes and stretching out her legs. "Old ladies hardly eat, and Mr. Pickens won't be home for a week. I don't need to shop."

Shopping disturbed her heart. She hadn't been to the open market in years. The endless hawkers calling "Mama, Mama" and sticking ripe tomatoes before her eyes disoriented her, so she stopped going. There was no point in it, and she could get everything she needed at the Indian Koshi's store. But Koshi unnerved her, too, with all that bowing, so she gave his boy her list and waited in the car while the order was assembled and packed. Willie paid Koshi every time he came home.

If she went to town, she would have to get dressed.

*

OKATCH was standing in the road when Mrs. Pickens returned from Koshi's store. He saluted and jogged after the car to the house. She switched off the engine, but remained in the car. She wished for one of those automatic door openers she'd seen in the Sears catalog so she could press a button and the left half of the house would open up and pull her in, Volkswagen and all, and shut him out. She would leave him baking on the driveway, slowly dissolving under his great coat.

She closed her eyes momentarily. When she opened them, the watchman's huge head filled the window. "Oh, help," she moaned and leaned on the horn. She was terrified of his flat face.

He jumped backwards and she grabbed her purse and escaped from the car.

"Go away." She swung her purse at him and opened the trunk. He reached over and grabbed two bags of groceries.

"Don't touch my food." She backed away. "Dorcas will get it."

He shifted the sacks in his arms and jogged towards the house, grinning.

"Leave them, I said."

She followed him to the kitchen.

He dropped the bags on the counter. "Everybody say Bwana Willie help us. Very good man, my boss."

"Mr. Pickens will not be home for one week." She folded her arms and glared at him.

His overcoat had no buttons and the frayed collar exposed several layers of fabric furled around his neck like a flower. His arms hung straight at his sides, and he wore canvas shoes with no socks and khaki pants that stopped an inch above his ankles. A narrow scar curved along his shin bone and disappeared in his shoe. "We must have car. Mama Willie, she help us." He squared his shoulders and waited.

Mrs. Pickens looked around for help. Dorcas gaped like Okatch, and Willie had been gone for days. "Not my car. I told you before, I cannot help you." The kitchen was narrow and hot. "I am sorry that my husband is not here," she said, gripping the counter. "Please go."

Okatch adjusted the lapel of his coat so it lay smoothly on his chest. "Yesterday you not have to help us. We did not need you." He shrugged his shoulders and opened his hands in a gesture of vulnerability. "Today, there is nobody else." He paused. "You must help us, Mama."

"Dorcas, tell him to go."

Mrs. Pickens hurried past them to the dining room. She closed the door and leaned against it. She couldn't help him. How could she transport a dead baby? The hospital was run by the Russians. In what condition would they release a dead child? Wrapped in a sheet? She was afraid of the germs, of the danger of infection. She didn't want to see the body. At least in Atlanta, it had been tidy and clean. They just took her baby away. Adelaide was a prune, all splotchy and stringy when she was alive. Mrs. Pickens never saw her dead.

She was trembling. "I need something." She went into the bathroom and stared at her pallid reflection in the mirror. "Della, you look like hell," she said. She took aspirin with codeine and lay down on the sofa.

*

HE WAS BACK at lunch time.

"Okatch is here," Dorcas said when she brought the tuna sandwich. "Do you want hot or cold tea?"

"Cold," Mrs. Pickens said. "Do we have ice?"

Dorcas nodded but didn't move towards the kitchen. She smoothed her apron over her skirt. "He talk to me," she said.

"Who?" Mrs. Pickens asked, stalling.

"Okatch say the hospital not give baby if they don't take her today."

"The baby is a girl?"

Dorcas nodded. "The family must have baby but he not find anybody to take her home," she said. "Bwana not come back?"

Mrs. Pickens took a bite of her sandwich and shook her head. "No, he's gone for the week." Or gone with his crew for the month. She never knew. She had been circling his days out on the calendar for two years to prove what her instinct told her, that his time home had sharply diminished. When he refused to sleep in the house and unrolled his moldy sleeping bag below the papaya tree every night he was in Kisumu, Mrs. Pickens became convinced that he had a mistress. A native slut, no doubt. How he humiliated her. She viewed the circled days on the calendar as mounting evidence and longed for him to question her markings and feared the day he would.

The sandwich was dry. She wondered if they were out of mayonnaise.

"He want to speak to you," Dorcas said. "He in the kitchen."

"Tell him to go away."

"He not go."

Mrs. Pickens wiped her mouth with a napkin. She stood up slowly and looked around the room. The doilies on the backs of the chairs in the sitting room were stained and the walls needed washing. The red cement floor gave everything the color of baked clay. Mrs. Pickens dropped her napkin on the table and walked to the kitchen door.

Okatch stood with his back to her, looking out the window. He waited until she was all the way in the room before he turned around.

"Mama, this is big problem. We must take baby today. Bus no take her." He dropped his head. "We have no money for taxi." He looked up to meet her eyes, but she turned away. "Bwana help us but he not here. You must drive car." He waited in her kitchen, holding his twisted stick, confident she would do the right thing. "You not have to take us far, but you must help us."

She looked out the back door. A dusty haze hovered over the yard. The row of pineapple tops Dorcas stuck in the ground behind the house had withered in the sun. The escarpment rose in the distance, faint and indistinct. Her mouth was dry. She filled a glass at the sink and drank slowly before turning towards Okatch. "Okay," she whispered, setting the glass down. "Let's do it now."

*

OUTSIDE, she climbed into the Volkswagen, slammed the door, and touched the steering wheel with her forehead. Okatch made no move to join her. She leaned on the horn and flapped her hand at him.

He opened the door and bent over her with warm, stale breath. "No, Mama, this car small. We take big car." He walked over to the Land Rover, leaving the VW door open. "We must have this car," he said, tapping the Rover fender.

Mrs. Pickens got out of the little car. "I can't drive that thing. I'm too small," she protested.

Okatch took a rag out of his pocket, spit into it, and wiped the side mirror. "I see you in this car before."

She felt like he had caught her in a lie. "I start it every couple of days, to let it run, so it won't die when Mr. Pickens is away. I don't drive it."

It was a long-wheel-base Land Rover, five doors, four-wheel drive, spare tire on the rear door and another on the hood. It had a roof rack and a pair of gallon water tins strapped to the front bumper. It would hold three of her Volkswagens, and it was filthy. When she started it for Willie, she had to perch on the edge of the seat to reach the pedals. It would be impossible for her to drive it to the end of her own driveway.

She folded her arms across her chest and faced Okatch. "I don't drive that car."

He shook his head and clicked his tongue in disapproval. "The little motor car not good," he said. "Shall we go in the big one?" He thumped the fender of the Land Rover as if he were selling it to her, got in, closed the door, and sat staring forward.

She slammed the door of the Volkswagen and went in the house. Dorcas was standing in the sitting room with her arms crossed, spying through the window. Mrs. Pickens glared at her and strode past. She pulled the keys to the Land Rover off the hook.

"Who does he think he is? I can't drive that car," she yelled and stormed out.

"Thank you, Memsahib," Dorcas called after her.

She climbed in the Land Rover and tried to pull the seat up. Okatch got behind her and pushed, and they inched it forward on the rusty runners. She held herself on the edge of the seat to depress the clutch and start the engine, glaring at Okatch.

"This car is too big for me."

"Yes, Mama. We go now."

She drove in first gear to the hospital. The guard at the gate nodded to Okatch and let them pass. They stopped at the back of the compound where fifteen or twenty people crowded around an area that looked like a loading dock.

"You wait here, Memsahib."

The people swarmed about Okatch when he got out of the car, talking and grabbing his arm as he climbed up the steps. He went through the door with two other men.

A woman with a child on her hip pointed at Mrs. Pickens in the Land Rover, and the crowd fell silent. A barefoot girl in a white skirt with a ragged hem walked over and stared at her. She had scars like claw marks on her cheeks. Mrs. Pickens rolled up the window, and the group surrounded the car. A boy about fourteen, wearing faded blue shorts and a green T-shirt that said Michigan State on the back, climbed on the right fender. Mrs. Pickens rapped on the windshield to get his attention, but he didn't turn around. A white-haired man with a bent stick that he used as a cane shouted at the boy and whacked him on the shins. The car rocked dangerously as the boy jumped down. Mrs. Pickens opened a newspaper and pretended to read.

She lowered the paper when Okatch shook the door handle. His solemn face filled the window. The other men held a wooden box, a meter long. The sight of the coffin leached the blood from Mrs. Pickens's body, and she felt faint.

"You open the door, please?" Okatch said. His voice was muffled and distant.

She nodded, breathing deeply, massaging her chest, then got out and walked around to unlock the rear door. The crowd shifted to the back of the car to watch the men slide the casket between the seats. A toothless woman grabbed her arm and pumped it, speaking rapid Luo.

"Don't!" Mrs. Pickens shrieked, shaking the woman off.

Okatch took the woman's arm. "This my mother," he said. A frail girl with round eyes and luminescent skin stepped forward. "And this my sister. She mother for baby."

The girl bowed and took Mrs. Pickens' hands. "Asante, Mama," she said. Then she tightened her lips and said thank you again.

Mrs. Pickens pulled her arm away, but nodded at the girl. She needed her dark glasses. The sun bounced off everything into her eyes. She seldom went anywhere without adequate eye protection.

The people started to pour into the Land Rover.

"Okatch, what are they doing? Stop them. I can't take all these people."

"This my family," he said. "Family of dead baby."

The Land Rover was loaded like a local bus, with people hanging out the windows and dangling from the side. The Michigan State boy had made himself comfortable on the roof rack and a younger boy sat in the spare tire on the hood. Two women were working with the rear door to prop it open to accommodate a third.

Mrs. Pickens's head wobbled on her thin neck. "This is dangerous, Okatch." She rubbed her clammy hands up and down her skirt. "I can't see out the window with that boy there."

"They must go with us."

"No, they will not go," she shouted. "How did they get here in the first place? They can take the bus." She got in the driver's seat and rolled down the window to glare at him. "The capacity of this vehicle is eight. Get the others out or we don't go."

She cranked the window up and stared straight ahead. The car smelled of sweat, native food, and animal skins. Voices behind her rose and fell, and the car swayed as people shifted places. She swallowed repeatedly. She was going to be sick.

At last, Okatch got in the seat beside her. "We ready now."

She turned around. His mother laughed and waved her hand, as if to say, let's go, let's go.

Mrs. Pickens clenched the steering wheel angrily. "Get your filthy hand out of my face," she said.

The woman bobbed her head, grinning broadly, and waved the hand again.

By the time they reached the hospital gate, she was able to press the gas pedal without hunching forward. She shifted into second gear when they crossed the white line north of the hospital that marked the equator and began the climb up the escarpment. She began panting and was alarmed by her rapid breathing and wanted to rub her chest, but was afraid to lift a hand from the steering wheel. She had never driven the Kakamega Road without Willie at the wheel. She felt that she was climbing at a twenty-degree incline, into air that was too thin and cool.

"Mama, we so happy for you," Okatch said.

"What do you mean, happy for me?"

"We so worried we no get baby home. We must bury Nekesa ourselves." He flicked the sweat off his forehead with two fingers. "You good, Mama, to help us. You drive this car that jumping like the toad, and you scared.

"How dare you say I'm frightened." The left tire sank in the soft shoulder and her hands slipped down the steering wheel, but she held it steady until she regained the road.

"You little and this motor car very big." Okatch smiled at her admiringly. "Don't worry, Mama. We take care of you like wife of chief. Everything be good." Then he leaned across her. "Turn there."

She stopped so abruptly that the engine died. He pointed to a rutted dirt road, the width of the Land Rover, that dropped off the shoulder of the highway and disappeared around a grassy hill. Two boys in blue shorts crisscrossed the path, chasing a frantic chicken. She looked at Okatch.

"Yes, this is the way."

"Is it far?"

"No."

She restarted the engine and eased onto the narrow road. The car jerked and coughed as her foot trembled on the clutch. She slammed on the brakes when the chicken flapped into her side window, and her passengers lurched forward. Somebody struck her on the head with an elbow.

She couldn't keep her sweaty hands on the steering wheel.

Okatch leaned out his window and shouted at the people who clogged the path, then touched her arm. "You can go now, Mama."

She dropped her head. "I can't."

"The people will move."

Slowly she released the clutch, and they lurched along the path. People and animals leapt to the side of the road as she approached. Somebody held a lamb in front of the windshield. A man with a spear jumped on the left bumper and rode for a few feet. She honked as he slid off, and her passengers howled.

The path had no shoulder, and she felt that hers was one of maybe ten vehicles that had ever used it. Willie had told her never to stop if she struck a pedestrian because the people would stone her. She was near tears. He should be here, she thought; it is him they want.

"Is good?"

Mrs. Pickens frowned. "You said twenty minutes."

"Yes, twenty minutes on the tarmac."

"I see. And how far now?"

"I not know. We never have motor car before."

She hit a deep rut and her hands flew off the steering wheel.

"We never take child to hospital before."

"Oh."

"No, but Nekesa, she very sick, and when doctor see her, he say she must stay. My sister, she cry, my mother, she cry, but I say look how clean, how nice in hospital. Medicine be good, I say."

She gunned the engine to cover the sound of his words. She didn't want to hear his story.

"My sister ask me what to do and I tell her something, but I don't know." He shook his head. "She think I know what to do."

Mrs. Pickens wheezed and hummed nervously under her breath.

His voice became halting and high pitched. "We stay outside all night. In morning we go in and a Kikuyu in a pink dress click her tongue when she see us. 'Bad news,' she say."

Mrs. Pickens nodded her head. Adelaide's nurse had worn a

white uniform and had a tiny hat pinned to her ratted hair, like a doll's cap caught in a wig. They couldn't save her, she had said.

"The baby dead, she say." Okatch shook his head slowly and moved his thin arm to the dashboard as if lifting a great weight. "She say we must take baby today," Okatch said softly.

Mrs. Pickens closed her mouth and the humming stopped.

"She know we have problem for car."

She slowed down. The road was so rutted, she couldn't keep her foot on the accelerator.

"Turn there."

She slammed on the brakes again. Her passengers yelped and surged forward, but Mrs. Pickens curved over the steering wheel and nobody hit her.

He pointed to a path a meter wide.

"I can't take this overloaded car down there," she said. "I'll take the baby a little farther, but that is all."

Okatch hesitated, then ordered everybody out. "They will walk. Me and baby go with you."

"And the child's mother," Mrs. Pickens said. "Let her ride."

The people streamed ahead of the Land Rover. As soon as their feet hit the ground, the women raised their voices an octave and cried and beat their breasts. Mrs. Pickens clutched the steering wheel. "Why are they wailing now?"

"They tell the people Nekesa coming."

In the nearly empty car, the casket slid and scraped along the floor with every bump or turn. Mrs. Pickens watched the mother in the mirror. The young woman tried to capture the box with her feet to keep it in one place. Finally, she straddled the coffin and held on with all fours. Mrs. Pickens drove as slowly as she could.

"How old was the child?"

"One year."

They crested a small rise that gave a view of the plains and Lake Victoria in the distance and entered a clearing, crowded with wailing people.

"You stop now," he said.

As soon as she got out of the car, three men met her at the rear door, lifted the casket out, and a procession of mourners formed to follow it down the far side of the hill. She stood by the car and watched them disappear.

A squat man wearing a khaki hat and a jacket with sleeves that covered his knuckles took both her hands and bowed.

"This my father," Okatch said.

His hand felt as bony as hers. She frowned at the sun and pulled her hand back to rummage through her purse for dark glasses. "I must go now," she said.

Okatch gasped, wide-eyed. "No. Now you eat. We give you food for your journey."

She smiled tightly and shook her head. "No, I am fine. Thank you." She turned to go. "You have a lot to do here."

Okatch spoke to his father, and the man grabbed her hand and stared at her intently, saying words she didn't understand. "You are his guest," Okatch explained. "You shame him if you go without food."

She could hear the undulating wail of the mourners below. Her eyes filled with tears, and she shook her head. "Oh," she said, wiping her eyes, "I don't belong here."

"Please, Mama. You help us very much. You stay."

Several children had gathered to stare at her. A regal woman with a brilliant red scarf twisted around her head grabbed Mrs. Pickens' hand, held it to her breast for an instant, bowed, and then released her to follow the sound of the wailing. The children filed by her shyly, grabbing her hand as the young woman had done, then followed the woman down the side of the hill. Mrs. Pickens held her hand to her own breast and turned in the direction of the wailing. She knew the droning voices of the mourners wouldn't stop until the child was buried. She knelt suddenly on the grass, then sat down. When Adelaide died, she and Willie met with the hospital chaplain and decided on cremation. There was no service.

She looked out at Lake Victoria spread across the valley below. She could see the long finger of the Kavirondo Gulf and the expanse beyond, looking like the ocean. The sun filled the lake with diamonds that moved when she turned her head. She thought that she saw the far edge of the water, where the great steamers Willie told her about docked. A light wind cooled her face and arms.

Okatch brought her a glass of milk.

"No, thank you," she said, politely. "Mr. Pickens says the milk here is tubercular."

"Is good milk. From cow today."

"No, I don't want it. The milk may be diseased." She pulled herself up on her knees. She ought to get up. "You know, germs, have sickness."

"Cow not sick." Okatch bowed and stiffly offered the glass again. "Take it, Mama."

She shook her head and looked around. Okatch stood before her, the glass resting on his flat right hand like a vase on a shelf. Finally, she sat back on the grass and accepted the milk. She touched it to her lips and smiled politely at Okatch. "Thank you." The milk was sweet and warm and soothed her throat like a toddy. She filled her mouth with warm milk and swallowed. She hadn't had a glass of milk since she was pregnant with Adelaide.

"Where is the child now?"

"The women wash and dress her." He paused. "My mother ask for you. Will you come?"

The sun was high overhead, but the air was cooler than in Kisumu. There was a low, rectangular house with a tin roof on the edge of the clearing that she guessed belonged to a chief of some sort. A short man wearing tight pants and a pith helmet stood in the doorway, scraping his teeth with a stick and watching two women carry food from the house to mats spread on the ground. When he tried to take a piece of bread from a passing plate, a woman, half his size, slapped his hand. Mrs. Pickens smiled to herself and nodded at Okatch. "Okay," she said and set her glass on the ground. She wiped her face with both hands and let him help her up.

He called to a girl about ten years old, and the three of them followed a narrow path, worn hard as macadam. The wailing was ahead. They arrived at a hut where several women squatted outside the door. One was grinding corn meal but the others were crying and swaying on their haunches. Okatch bowed to them, and Mrs. Pickens entered the hut with the girl. She stood blinking, trying to see in the dim light. In the middle of the room a low fire burned under a large pot of water. The grandmother was dipping cloths in the kettle and handing them to the mother who bent over something. The girl put her hand on Mrs. Pickens' back and gently pushed her towards the mother.

There was the child, spread on a mat as if she were sleeping. Mrs. Pickens squatted beside the young mother and touched her arm. The girl nodded, then continued bathing the child and weeping. The grandmother gave her a cloth and put her hand on the child. Mrs. Pickens stroked the dead baby's arm with the warm cloth and began to hum in a low voice. Other women sat along the wall of the hut, swaying and crying and talking to themselves. The room was dark, with only the light from the door and the fire. The smell of burning eucalyptus filled the air like incense. The child's thick hair lay damp on her head, and her body was as smooth as the inside of a shell. The sunlight streaming through the door illumined her.

"She is a beautiful baby," Mrs. Pickens whispered.

The young mother looked up at her, eyes full, and said, "Yes?" in English.

"Maridadi toto."

The mother put her head on Mrs. Pickens' shoulder and wept. She knelt awkwardly on the dirt floor and buried her head in the young woman's neck. They cried, holding the damp cloths and each other. Mrs. Pickens whispered, "My daughter died, too, a long time ago."

The grandmother came up behind them, holding a small stool. "Memsahib."

Mrs. Pickens wiped her eyes and pulled herself up. She was stiff, but she sat on the stool to watch the mother. The girl kissed her hand and turned back to the baby. The grandmother joined her daughter bathing the child.

After several minutes Mrs. Pickens took her stool and moved to the edge of the hut. Two toothless old women, wrapped in kanga cloth and smelling like smoke, made room for her, smiling and nodding as she found her place. They went back to beating their breasts and wailing. She leaned against the wall with them, closed her eyes, and saw her own beautiful, wrinkled baby behind her eyelids. She put her head on her lap and wept for Adelaide.

*

WHEN the baby was prepared, she followed the other women behind Okatch and the father of the child. They held the casket aloft and all the people leapt and jumped and wailed and called the child's name, "Nekesa, Nekesa, Nekesa." They buried her in a mound on the edge of the escarpment. The sun was in Mrs. Pickens' eyes as she looked towards the lake. All she could see was light and the shadows of people around her.

Okatch took her by the elbow and they walked back to his father's house. He asked her to come in the hut, for five minutes, please, and she followed him. She felt soft inside, as if she had just soaked in a warm bath. She sat on a chair and waited. A girl of about five brought her bread, then leaned against her and stroked her arm. The child put her hand next to Mrs. Pickens' and laughed, then ran back to her mother.

Finally, Okatch appeared. "You can go now," he said.

She rose stiffly and walked to the door. She turned and nodded at the people watching her, then stepped out into the bright sunlight.

His father was waiting at the car, brandishing a live chicken. She shook her head when she saw him, but he grinned and waved the chicken. It squawked and tried to peck his hand.

"This for you, Mama. For bringing the baby," Okatch said.

Mrs. Pickens shuddered and shielded her eyes with her hand. "Oh, no," she said. "I am afraid of chickens. You don't have to give me anything."

Okatch laughed as if she had told a joke. "We very happy for you to help us."

He opened the back door of the Land Rover and his father tossed the chicken in. The bird fluttered to the top of the passenger seat.

Okatch and his father watched Mrs. Pickens closely. She realized that she was stuttering and talking to herself and she covered her mouth with her right hand.

"How can I drive with a chicken in the car?"

"It good chicken. Fine dinner for you and Bwana Willie."

Okatch took her free hand in his and bowed. Then he opened the door and she climbed in. She started the engine, and the chicken flew up against the roof, squawking, and then she couldn't find it in the mirror.

"Oh, mercy," she said, covering her face.

Okatch knocked on the window. She looked at him and smiled, then laughed. She was still smiling as she waved to the two men, put the car in gear, and jerked across the clearing. She followed the same narrow path, people scattering before her. It was a familiar journey. She stopped once to look behind her but it was as if a curtain had closed across the road. A single woman with an umbrella balanced across her head stood sideways in the path, watching her.

*

IT WAS DUSK when she stopped the car in front of her house. She couldn't see the chicken when she looked back but she sensed its heart beating. She bent around her seat and saw the bird in the far corner of the Land Rover, crouched behind the tire iron. Mrs. Pickens set her purse on the passenger seat and made her way to the back of the car, crooning in her breathy voice. She squatted before the last seat and reached blindly for the chicken. It was warm and soft and came easily when she pulled it forward. She curled her fingers around the bird's legs and held it under her left arm, next to her breast. She heard the bird panting and felt its heart with her fingers. She picked up her purse, got out of the car and walked to the house, talking to the chicken, slowing the rapid beating of both their wild hearts.

Miss Clay County 1960

AFTER NINETEEN YEARS at the front register at Bolton's Drug Store on the square in Clintock, Irene could watch a man frown over perfume bottles and know which one he'd buy; she could tell who was having an affair or neglecting their mother by the cards brought to her register; she knew which kids tore coupons out of comic books, exactly how much money they carried in their pockets and whether or not they'd buy bubble gum on impulse at the counter. She felt it was within her authority to refuse to sell a child inappropriate merchandise. "Too close to dinner time," she'd say, tapping the child's hand in the caramels with her long fingernail.

When the shopping center was built out on Highway 41, Bolton's lost a few customers but Irene still knew the face, the walk, the gesture of each person that pushed through the glass doors.

"Good morning, Myrna," she'd say. "Out of cough medicine?"

"How'd you know that?"

"Your mama needs chapstick, Buddy."

"Yes'm. It's on her list."

So when she saw the back of a stranger's head through the Ziggy cards, she was startled. She hadn't seen him come in and didn't recognize the pale hair pulled across the crown of the head. He stood between the card racks but didn't move like a card browser: head up to survey the rack, down to read a card, then up and searching again. His head turned sharply, swiftly towards the back where Cecil Bolton, owner/pharmacist, was preparing a prescription. He walked down to the gift wrap and Irene caught his profile — no eyebrows, thin nose, hard mouth. He paused at the end of the aisle then faced her and nodded. She quickly looked away. He was going to rob the store. There was a gun in his pocket. Without moving her head, she dialed the police on the phone concealed below the counter.

"Captain Walnut."

"Robbery in progress at Bolton's Drug Store," she whispered.

"Who is this?"

"Shhh," she hissed. Walnut's voice resonated through the store. "Irene Campbell."

The phone went dead.

She redialed the number.

"Irene, that you?"

"Yes, sir," she whispered. The man was in profile to her, his small eye flat against his head, watching her. She rubbed her forehead as if she had a headache, to make him think she was on a personal call. "There's a criminal in here," she whispered, "looking at Ziggy cards."

"He got a gun to your head?"

"Not yet."

"Call me back when he does." The connection died against her ear.

The man thrust a card and a dollar bill at her. His fingers were thin as bones and his nails were a quarter inch too long.

She rang it up. "That's a dollar six with tax."

He fished in his left pocket and she held her breath, watching his hand curve over the revolver.

"You got a gun?" she asked.

The man winked and dropped a dime in her palm. "Put the change in your penny box," he said. "I don't need a bag for the card." He pulled it out of her hand and was gone before she counted out the four cents.

She threw the pennies in the box.

Cecil came up a minute later. "I got to leave early today, Irene. You close up for me?" It was ten to six.

"There was a stranger in here just now, bought a card. He's coming back to rob us," Irene said.

"Yeah," said Cecil. "Thanks for closing."

She followed him to the door and locked it, shaking her head at the teenage boy with his hand on the door. One of the Blum boys wanting cigarettes, she thought. He slapped the door with the heel of his hand and made an obscene gesture at her. She drew the shade and turned off the overhead light.

She liked the peace of the store after closing. She began her evening routine by misting her cash register with Lysol. Then she sprayed the telephone, the film rack, the cigarette dispenser, and the rubber pad she stood on. She would have sprayed the candy bars but Cecil said he'd fire her if she so much as pointed her aerosol can in that direction, so she dusted the wrappers with an orange feather duster and turned each package so the product name faced out. She scrubbed the day's fingerprints off the magazine rack and ran a knife under all the shelves, patrolling for gum. When the store was in perfect order, she called the police. It was seven o'clock.

"Sergeant Walnut."

"Clyde, this is Irene. I'm leaving."

Walnut didn't say anything.

"You got a squad car coming by?"

"As usual, Irene."

"Be sure they look in," she said. "That robber's coming back."

Walnut had already hung up. She sighed loudly and wiped the phone again, then switched on the burglar alarm and left through the back hallway.

"I was sinking deep in sin, far from the peaceful shore . . ."

Irene sang as she climbed the stairs to her two rooms over the store. She filled the empty stairwell with a familiar hymn every night to carry her safely home to her baby, Rae Jean.

". . . Very deeply stained within, sinking to rise no more . . ."

When she stopped to catch her breath, she heard a radio playing rock music. She closed her eyes and sighed like Martha, chastened by Jesus Christ Himself. Irene particularly admired Martha, the woman-Job she called her — no saint but a hard worker.

". . . But the Master of the seas, heard my despairing cry . . ."

She smelled fresh cigarette smoke. She could ignore that too.

". . . From the waters lifted me, now safe am I . . ."

She went up three more steps, turned the corner, and stopped singing. A wide beam of light spread out from her doorway. She clutched her chest and screamed. A stabber had bashed in the door. Rae Jean was supposed to keep the door locked and now she lay dead and violated under the kitchen table.

"Help me, Lord," Irene hollered and hurried up the last steps, clutching the railing. "Rae Jean? Answer me, Baby." At the top of the stairs, she fell against the door frame.

Her daughter sat at the kitchen table, drinking Tab and smoking a cigarette. Irene gasped at the sight of her, unable to speak.

"God, Mama, you'll wake the dead." Rae Jean stubbed out her cigarette and looked up.

"Our door is supposed to be locked," Irene yelled.

"I found that," Rae Jean said, pointing to a yellowed newspaper clipping stuck on the refrigerator door.

"Tell me why this door is standing wide open, Missy. Any kind of trash could walk right in and stab us in our beds."

Rae Jean laughed and made an exaggerated show of looking around the room. "You see anybody in bed?"

Irene slammed the door, hooked the chain, and positioned herself between her daughter and the refrigerator. The cat jumped off the counter and rolled over on her foot.

"That ain't the point," she said. She tripped over the cat as she squeezed past her daughter to the bedroom they shared. The animal ran ahead of her and jumped up on the dresser. Three of her drawers stood open and the blue shelf paper that lined her underwear drawer was creased up and over the lip of the chest. The clipping had been under that paper. Irene blinked slowly and took a deep breath, then another. She wanted to kick the bureau, slam the drawers shut, and throw herself across the bed; instead she pushed the cat off the dresser and sat down to untie her shoes.

She was in the bathroom, rinsing out her stockings, when Rae Jean turned the radio up.

"Turn that thing down," Irene hollered.

The music stopped suddenly, and she heard the radio scrape across the table. When she went back to the kitchen, Rae Jean sat hunched and sullen on the corner of the table.

"Don't sit on the table. We got chairs." She rattled the door handle to make sure it was locked.

"Why'd you never tell me about that?" Rae Jean nodded toward the clipping. It was a picture of Irene at nineteen, in a strapless formal with the sash of a beauty contest winner across her dress. Her head was bent over a bunch of roses cradled in her arms.

Irene turned on the hot water and leaned over the sink, eyes closed, steaming her face as she filled a chipped basin. She turned off the water but bent into the steam, softening her skin, smoothing away ugly wrinkles. "It was a long time ago and it wasn't much then," she said when she straightened up. She shook a lump of Epsom Salts in the water and put the basin on the floor.

"Not much?" Rae Jean slapped the table. "Mama, you were Miss Clay County. You were a beauty queen. I never even knew you were from Johnsonville."

"I don't know what you're getting so excited about. It makes no difference now," Irene said. She got out the instant coffee and dug through the dishes in the sink until she found a cup. "You ever think about washing these dishes?"

When her coffee was ready, she sat down, slipped her feet into the hot water, closed her eyes, and took a deep, luxurious breath. "Thank you, Lord, for this day," she said. Then she raised the cup to her chin, steaming her face, and smiled at Rae Jean, "Hand me the sugar, Baby."

Rae Jean slid the sugar across the table, carelessly enough to show that she was upset but carefully enough that Irene couldn't find fault. She pushed the other chair back with her foot and sat across from Irene. "It does make a difference," Rae Jean said, leaning back. "If I'd of known you were a beauty queen, I could of held my head up in this town. I'd be somebody."

"I see," Irene said. "You been ashamed of me." She stood up, her feet still in the basin, and yanked the clipping off the refrigerator. She looked like Rae Jean in the picture — big eyes, thick hair that she'd tried to tame by teasing it. She stood at an angle to the camera, left foot slightly ahead of the right and turned just so, a model's pose she'd seen in a magazine. Her mouth was too big, lips too full, but the photographer had liked her Anita Ekberg pout. Don't spoil your face laughing, he'd said, be stingy showing those gorgeous teeth and when you do smile, you'll blind the judges. Rae Jean had the same wide eyes, green instead of hazel, with straight red hair that she let hang limp, and a dimple in her chin.

105

"What you doing, messing with my stuff?" Irene said. "You got no call to go through my dresser drawers."

"Why do we live like this if you really won that contest?"

Irene smiled at her daughter. "Don't smoke so much, Baby. It causes wrinkles." She stretched across the table for her daughter's arm, but Rae Jean moved out of reach. "Wouldn't have changed a thing," Irene said. " 'Beauty is vain: but a woman that feareth the Lord, she shall be praised.' " She sipped her coffee. "Winning that kind of thing don't mean crackers."

"But if people knew, it might get us some respect," Rae Jean said, chewing on her lip and staring at the wall.

"Did you have supper, Baby?"

"You aren't listening to me!" Rae Jean struck the table with her fist, pushed her chair into the table and stomped past Irene. "I hate this dump!" she shrieked and slammed the bedroom door behind her.

The Evangelical Association calendar fell off the door. Irene picked it up and stared at the illustration for July. She would like to immerse her feet in the stream in that picture. The sun shone on the water, clear and clean, and the new grass along the shores was soft. Rae Jean would feel good in a place like that, Irene thought, where the air was sweet and only the birds of the forest and the lilies of the field would surround them. Irene wasn't a church-goer, but she believed in the good news of the gospel that she heard Sunday morning on television.

She took a dish towel off the oven door and dried her feet, then pulled the hair pins out of her French twist, shaking her hair around her shoulders. Her brush was in the bathroom and she didn't want to go through the bedroom to get it — she'd let Rae Jean sulk for a while — so she combed through her teased hair with her fingers and drank her coffee. She tilted the toaster oven on two legs so she could peer into the black glass. Her hair was graying along the swatch she'd bleached for the contest. People said she lost at state because the roots showed through in the streak but that had nothing to do with it, nothing at all. It was the judging.

She shook her head and used the corner of the dish towel to wipe her eyes without smearing her mascara, then folded the clipping, slipped it between two sections of the morning paper and put it in the garbage. She made herself another cup of coffee and was rubbing lotion on her legs when the bedroom door opened.

Rae Jean leaned on the door frame, twisting her long hair around a scarf and stabbing hairpins at it. She wore a pink mini-skirt and a sleeveless, white blouse. "You know what they call you, Mama?"

Irene stared at her, suddenly aware of her daughter's beauty. Rae Jean's lips were the deep rose of late raspberries, even without lipstick, and her unlined face filled with color as she stared angrily at her mother. I was like that once, Irene thought.

"They call you the Painted Desert, Mama," Rae Jean was shouting at her and crying at the same time. "You wear all that stupid make-up, like you're trying to get some damn new face every morning, and you're always talking about robbers and stabbers to people. Everybody says you're crazy."

Irene nodded — she had heard it all — and opened her arms to her daughter, but Rae Jean threw the last hair pin on the floor and pushed past her to the hallway. By the time Irene stood up, she heard the door slam at the street level. She stretched across the kitchen sink to look out the window and saw her daughter crossing the square on the diagonal, her hair already falling down, the scarf trailing.

She switched on the light over the sink and turned on the lamp in the bedroom and the fluorescent tube in the bathroom, leaving the shades up as if she thought Rae Jean would be attracted to light like a June bug. When she saw her face in the bathroom mirror, she was surprised that her cheeks were wet. She undressed, put on her pajamas, her bathrobe, her slippers, slowly, to pass the time, and picked up the Daily Devotionals from her night stand and went back to the kitchen table to wait.

*

IT was midnight when she heard laughter across the street. She switched off the kitchen light so she could stand at the window unobserved. Rae Jean was not alone. Irene heard their voices, then the sandpaper rubbing of shoes on the pavement. A man said, "Hey, Beautiful, don't do me that way."

Irene closed her eyes to hear better. A car accelerated across the square. The fluorescent bulb in the bathroom hummed. Irene held her watch up to her eye. Twelve seventeen. She leaned to the window but couldn't see anything. "Rae Jean, that you?"

Somebody gasped and she heard the sputter of stifled laughter.

"Rae Jean, get on up here or I'm coming down."

She stepped back from the window, her arms folded tightly across her chest, and waited. Finally she heard Rae Jean on the stairs. Irene turned on the light, picked up a nail file, and sat down.

A minute later Rae Jean came in.

"Where you been?" Irene looked up from her nails. Rae Jean's skin was raw around the lips, her blouse hung out of her skirt, and her hair had the unkempt look of somebody who'd just climbed out of bed. "I been worried sick and you look like you been in a wrestling match."

Rae Jean crossed to the sink, filled a glass with water, and drank it with her back to her mother. "I went to the show," she said.

"You been with a man."

Rae Jean set the glass in the sink and turned around. "Yes, ma'am, I have been with a man. I am eighteen years old and I have been with a man. Yes, ma'am." She licked her lips and bit the corner of her mouth. "I can go with a man any time I want, Mama. I can go with two men. I can go with three. I am growed up." She turned back to the sink and filled her glass again.

"Shut your mouth." Irene stood up and leaned across the table, pointing the file at Rae Jean's back. "You don't know what you're saying. You're talking like a tramp." Tears stood in her eyes and she started to cough, clutching her heart with the hand holding the nail file thrust between her fingers. She felt like she'd been stabbed. "I raised you better than that."

"Yeah." Rae Jean held out a cigarette to her mother.

Irene slapped her hand down and fell back in the chair.

"You raised me good. Just one little problem." Rae Jean leaned back and inhaled deep into her lungs, then blew the smoke out as if she parted with it reluctantly. "Who in the hell was my daddy?"

"We aren't talking about that."

"I am," Rae Jean shouted.

"You don't speak to your mama that way," Irene whispered fiercely. She started to hum and shake her head and tap her fingers on the table to the slow beat of a hymn. Her face was red, as if she'd been struck.

Rae Jean doused her cigarette under the faucet. "I don't believe that lie you tell everybody — killed in a truck accident. What's his damn name?"

" 'I will sing the wondrous story . . .' " Irene sang under her breath.

"Stop singing them damn hymns and look at me, Mama." Rae Jean's voice was low and calm. "I got a right to know who my daddy was."

Irene leaned across the table, tears in her eyes, to face her daughter. " 'Of the Christ who died for me . . .' "

"He wasn't killed in no accident, was he?"

" 'How He left his home in glory . . .' " Irene sang.

"Shut up, Mama, just shut up that singing and tell me." Rae Jean grabbed Irene by the shoulder and shook her.

Irene pushed her off. " 'For a cross at Calvary,' " she sang. " 'Oh, yes, I'll sing the wondrous story . . .' "

"Mama, if you weren't married, it don't matter to me. Did you love him a lot?"

Irene stopped singing. "Your daddy ain't about love." She coughed and pulled at the collar of her robe.

"Tell me, Mama."

Irene stood up. "I'm going to bed."

Rae Jean shoved the table into her mother, pinning Irene against the refrigerator. "I got to know. Now. You sit down and tell me."

Irene looked at her daughter. "You're just like him, pushing people around, slamming and pushing and hurting."

Rae Jean's face was red and sweaty. She touched her mother on the arm, but Irene shook her off.

"I don't know his name," Irene shouted. She sat down, closed her eyes, covered her ears, and bent over the table. "I can't tell you because I don't know his name."

Rae Jean took the other chair and sat down.

"Tell me anyway."

Irene shook her head.

"Tell me."

Irene kept her eyes closed and spoke into her hands. Her voice sounded muffled and unfamiliar.

"I'd never been nowhere, never been out of Clay County 'til that beauty contest and there was this preliminary interview. The other judge, a woman, got sick, and so it was just me and him — this man from Atlanta."

Rae Jean hit the table and turned away. "And you slept with him for the damn contest."

Irene looked up sharply. "He told me to walk across the room so he could see how I moved so I did and he shook his head like I done something wrong and he stood up and held me on the shoulder and here with his other hand." She curved her red nails at the seat of her robe and walked across the kitchen swinging her hips. "He told me to walk like this and I said I'd practice later, but he made me do it again and again and again and then he locked the door." She stopped and bent over the sink, her head moving from side to side. "I didn't know what to do, Rae Jean, I just didn't know. He was a big man and had this expensive suit on."

"Oh, shit, Mama. He raped you."

Irene pressed her face against the cool refrigerator with her back to Rae Jean and started to cry. "He made me take off my stockings and then he tied my hands with one and my mouth with the other." She glanced at Rae Jean. "We didn't have panty hose back then," she said and tried to smile. Rae Jean's face was white and she was crying. "I'm sorry, Baby. I never told nobody," Irene whispered. "I didn't know what to do."

Rae Jean struck the table with her hand. Then she stood up and put her arms around her mother. Rae Jean was soft and smelled like violets in the rain. "It's okay, Mama. You did nothing wrong."

Irene pushed her face into Rae Jean's white blouse. "I'm so sorry," she said, "I'm just so sorry."

*

SHE woke at six the next morning with a headache, puffy eyes, and a crick in her neck. Rae Jean was curled around her pillow, snoring softly. She smiled at her daughter and stroked the tangled red hair. She kissed her on the shoulder. "Time to go to work, Baby," she whispered and slipped out of bed. She dressed quickly and shook Rae Jean again.

Then she went out to the kitchen and began sectioning a grapefruit. The kitchen was bright with sunlight. She rubbed the cat's belly with her toe and dropped a piece of grapefruit on the floor for her.

When Rae Jean came out, ready for work, Irene smiled at her happily. "I'm going to get my eyes lifted. I look worse than Elizabeth Taylor." She picked up the jar of coffee and shuffled across the linoleum to get the hot water. "Get yourself a cup, Baby." She flipped the top off the teapot with a knife because the knob was missing and the lid was too hot to touch.

"Why don't you use that kettle I gave you for Christmas? We should have something nice in here."

"I'm saving it." Irene filled both cups.

"You're getting senile, boiling water in that rotten aluminum."

"It'll take more'n hot water to make me crazy." Irene pulled her skin taut along the eye bone with her left hand, making her face lopsided. "My eyes are about to sag permanently closed. I believe I'll go to Dr. Vaneer."

"God, Mama, he costs a fortune. You worry about your looks too much."

"Did I tell you the girl at Sears asked me if I dyed the streak in my hair, it was so perfect?"

"You're wasting our money."

"Would you rather I sent another check to the Evangelicals?"

"Same thing."

Rae Jean picked up the cat and stood at the window.

Irene stared at her dim reflection in the toaster oven. If she stopped trying to be pretty, she might as well lie down and let the Lord take her. She smoothed the folds of skin on her neck and her eyes filled with tears. She glanced at Rae Jean's rigid back and the cat's baby face resting on her shoulder and smiled at the cat's wild purring. What did an animal know? She held her breath. She ought to tell Rae Jean to run as fast as she could, while she was young and had hope, run right out of Clintock, cross the county line, and find some place where a woman could live her life warm and safe as a cat. A siren sounded across the square and Irene lifted her head. Somebody was coming up the stairs.

"Wonder who that is?" she said.

Rae Jean let the cat drop. "Got to go, Mama." Her hand grazed Irene's shoulder. "I might be late tonight."

Irene leapt up and opened the door, stepping out into the hall. There was a man coming up the stairs. "What you want?" she said.

"I come for Rae Jean." It was the same voice she'd heard in the street the night before.

"Mama."

"Stay in the house, Rae Jean."

Rae Jean pushed through the door and stood beside Irene. "This is Clark. He's giving me a ride to work."

"You too good for the bus?"

The man advanced one step on the stairs.

"Stay where you are, young man. Rae Jean, you come in the house."

Rae Jean didn't move. "I'm going to work, Mama. Clark is giving me a ride to the plant and he's picking me up after and we're going to the show."

"No, you aren't."

"Goodbye, Mama."

She slapped Rae Jean across the cheek with the back of her hand. "No!" she shrieked, lifting her hand to hit her again.

"Mama!" Rae Jean hollered.

She felt her daughter's breath across her face, a powerful, wet wind, then heard her feet, and the man's, hitting the stairs and the thud of the door slamming shut at the bottom. Her hand tingled as if it had been asleep. She covered her face with it and backed into the kitchen, pulling the door closed after her.

*

SHE was still at the kitchen table with her head on her arms when Cecil knocked on the door. "Irene?" he said. "You in there? Time to open up."

She got half-way downstairs before she realized she still had her slippers on. She went back slowly to get her shoes.

The thief came in just as she opened up the register. His coat was buttoned to the neck and she only saw the back of his head as he walked past her, took a left at the comic books, and went to the display of Dr. Scholl's foot preparations. Opchurch, the lawyer, stopped in for cigarettes and Irene lost track of the man who'd rob the store.

"How's your daughter, Miz Campbell?"

"She's getting along real good," Irene said and gave him his change, looking past him at the man holding a candy bar. The stranger smiled at her. She pulled the phone close and dialed the first six digits of Walnut's number. The store was empty except for Cecil reading the paper and smoking his pipe at the back register. She could smell the tobacco and hear the rustle of the newspaper.

He threw the candy on the counter and held out a ten dollar bill. The corner of the bill trembled, and when Irene gingerly tugged at the end nearest her, the man didn't let go. They stood there, bound to each other by the money, Irene pulling, the man holding steady. She jerked it again, but his grip was firm. He smiled, exposing a quarter inch of his top teeth, then leaned across the counter and spoke so close to her that his breath touched her face. "Empty the cash register in a bag."

He put his hand in his right pocket. She heard the click of the safety on the pistol and slyly punched the last number of the police station. She concealed the receiver against her thigh and felt the vibrations of the ring.

She rang up the sale with her left hand and the cash register drawer shot open. On her thigh the ringing stopped and Walnut's voice said, "Hello. Hello? Hello?" Click.

"Now, lady."

She dropped the dead phone on the floor and looked to the rear of the store but couldn't see Cecil. "You want all this money?" she asked loudly.

"Yes, ma'am." He smiled pleasantly. "You know what I have in my pocket?"

She wanted to look away from him but he held her eyes like a cobra. She tried to blink but her tear ducts were sucked dry. "Don't bind up my mouth," she said.

He looked to the back of the store then out the window. They both saw Opchurch coming back. The man lifted his hand in the pocket. "Fill the bag."

She shook her head and tears started to come. She clutched the cash register with both hands and shook it. "You ain't getting nothing," she said.

But he didn't hear her. He spread his giant hand across her breasts and shoved her into the cigarette rack, then pushed her again when she tried to straighten up. He came behind the counter and she hit his jaw but he backed her into the wall, holding her there with his heavy body so she couldn't move while he pulled all the money into his bag. He shoved her to the floor as he left. "Bitch," he said.

She jumped up and ran after him, pushing past Opchurch, out into the street. "Thief!"

The man dismissed her with a wave of his arm, got into a small yellow car, and drove away. People on the sidewalk stared and walked slowly around her as if she were on an island.

"Stop him!" she yelled.

The Blum boy, lounging on the hood of his convertible in front of the shoe store next door, whistled, "Hey, Painted Desert. Getting any?" His girlfriend giggled.

Irene looked down at her broken fingernails and stuck her fists in her arm pits.

"Go on in the store, Irene," Opchurch said, stepping around her, but she didn't move.

She couldn't go back behind that narrow counter. She sat down on the curb and squeezed her legs together. She pressed her head down, plugging her eye sockets with her knees and wrapped her arms around her legs.

"Call Rae Jean," somebody said.

"Call Walnut."

"Naw, ain't nothing happened."

The Blum boy beat out a rat-a-tat-tat on his horn and backed into the traffic circling the square, but Irene didn't hear him or look up.

Handyman

HOMER STOOD BEHIND THE TWO-WAY MIRROR watching Myrna
Smythe, the mail carrier, tell a Vietnamese woman to take her
cleaning elsewhere. "Homer only deals with certain kinds of dirt,"
Myrna said, not unkindly. The woman stared up at Myrna, then
searched for Homer through the mirror with her deep civet eyes
before she slowly pulled her clothes off the counter and backed out
of the shop. Homer emerged a minute later, reluctantly, hoping that
Myrna would ignore the incident.

"Law says you got to serve them all, but I won't tell," she said,
slapping his mail on the counter.

"My cash register isn't working right," he explained quickly.

"Ain't it hard on business, not waiting on strangers?" Myrna
dragged her husband's Sunday suit out of the mail bag and dropped
it on the stack of magazines.

"I didn't know her," Homer said, pulling the suit towards him to
fold the coat inside out. He liked to protect the finish of a garment
before it was cleaned. He nodded at the cash register. "It's eating
the tape."

"Yeah," she said. She leaned over the machine and pushed keys
randomly while he wrote out the claim check. The register drawer

shot open and Myrna snorted and tapped Homer on the shoulder with her big fist. "It works," she said. She was six two, same as Homer, but outweighed him by fifty pounds.

Homer was a loose-jointed man, with arms that swung too easily, as if the shoulder sockets weren't snapped in securely. He wore the plaid bell bottoms Buddy Pittman forgot when he was drafted in 1968 and a burgundy V-neck sweater, extra large, that was left in winter storage for two years. He had a chronic sniffle and was twenty by the time he graduated from high school because his mother kept him home every time he sneezed. He developed a weepy-eye condition that year, after she burned to death the morning their house burst into flames. He saw it go up as he turned the corner on his paper route, the only job she ever let him have. Doc Profett said his dripping eyes were caused by stress and allergies and scheduled skin patch tests for him, but Homer canceled the appointment. He moved his bed and drafting table into the back of his mother's cleaners and sold the charred house to his first customer the next day.

Over the years he ordered various types of shelving units. Every patch of his living space was organized, and his books, tools, catalogs, magazines, paper plates and cups were neatly stacked or filed around the swivel arm chair in the center of the room. Homer was too tall for the room, even in his hunched stance. He had to bend his knees at the door and slip into the chair so he wouldn't bump into his Moments in History, miniature dioramas suspended by fish line from the low ceiling. He had started the series of tableaux, quite naturally, with the battle for Kennesaw Mountain, June 27, 1864, at 9:25 a.m. He and his mother used to drive to the top of the mountain with a picnic lunch every Sunday afternoon. They'd hike the three hundred yards from the parking area to the summit, both of them wheezing from their allergies. When she got her breath, his mother would say:

— My great granddaddy's blood is in this soil.

— Yes'm.

They'd stand together, gazing at the grassy hills below:

— He fell just there, Homer, fighting for the Confederacy.

She'd start to cry and point to a scooped-out indentation that indicated a trench:

— He was looking up at General Joseph Johnston himself when

that Yankee bullet cut him down in the prime and pride of his manhood.

That was the moment Homer captured in his miniature: his blood ancestor, young Virgil Hughs, staring respectfully at the general on the ridge, his body half-turned and arching from the Yankee bullet in his back, his eyes clear and calm from looking at a general, but his mouth forming the wide, round OH of a dead man. Homer had trouble with the arms — was he saluting? was he holding a gun? He finally left them hanging, like his own heavy limbs, caught between duty and personal salvation.

Myrna grabbed his wrist. "What you oughta do is move out to Clintock Mall where the customers are and get a register with a scanner like Winn-Dixie. Everything here is older than Moses."

He jerked his arm back and frowned. "I was twelve and a half when Mama bought that register — March 4, 1957." He snapped open the machine and peered inside. He knew how to replace the tape and had, in fact, inserted three new rolls since Monday morning, but each had been consumed.

"It can be fixed," he said. He was pleased that Myrna was there on the other side of the counter. He felt like discussing his course of action and was only comfortable speaking to people he'd known all his life. "Can you recommend a repairman?"

"Repair person," Myrna said and pawed through her mail sack. After a minute she located a yellow post card. "I can't let you have this, but get the number off it." She gave him the card. "Probably nigger or foreign but you oughta be able to tell when you call. That's another reason to move out to the mall."

He looked at the card. Under a hammer crossed with a wrench, he read:

"Handyman-Jack-of-all-trades: If it's broken we fix it — FAST and REASONABLE."

He wrote the number down, then turned to Myrna with satisfaction. "The term Jack-of-all-trades was first used in 1618 by a Geffray Mynshul in his treatise entitled *Essays and Characters from Prison*."

"Yeah, Homer." She grabbed the card, buried it in her pouch, and walked out, ringing a bell as she stepped on a soft place in the carpet.

Homer had the doorbells installed in the floor January 11, 1986, after that African scared him so badly. He had been sitting at the TV tray behind the counter, working on Scarlett O'Hara as she plunged down the staircase, her arms flung before her, the long eyelashes plastered against the eyelids and her concave cheeks forcing all her breath through her round, red lips, when a voice boomed, "Please, I have some dirty clothes." Homer's head snapped back and he broke the dental scaler he used for chiseling in facial details. He dropped a dish towel over the sculpture and stood up.

A black man with claw marks on his forehead stood on the other side of the counter. "I want to leave my clothes," he said, showing wide, white teeth. The man was dressed in a gown that hung from his shoulders, blue, white, and brown stripes, embroidered around the neck and closed with elaborate frogs. A round cap sank in his thick hair.

"Uh, no," Homer said, "Only American clothes here." He smiled his thin-lipped smile and escaped behind the two-way mirror.

The man refused to leave. "Come now," he called to Homer. "I just want these clothes to be cleaned."

Homer covered his ears.

"Come, man, take my clothes."

Homer didn't move.

"I bought these shirts at K-Mart."

Homer squatted behind the mirror, eyes closed. He expected the black man to leap over the counter and come looking for him. When he finally stood up to peer through the trick mirror, the shop was empty. Still, he thought the man could be crouched behind the counter or flattened on the north wall. He wasn't able to breathe normally until he had examined every part of the shop. He was alone. He locked the door, pulled the shades, and put his "closed" sign out. It was after that scare that he hung a cow bell on the door and mined the small waiting area with under-the-carpet door bells, installed randomly so that nobody could avoid tripping one of them.

*

HE SAW the handyman hurrying across the street, a thin man in a pressed beige uniform and cap, carrying a satchel of tools, striding with the confidence of a professional. Homer smiled. He knew what to expect of a person whose dress was appropriate to the job.

He waited behind the mirror and stepped out, blushing, when the doorbells announced the arrival of the repairman.

"Good morning," Homer said. "You've come about the cash register?"

The handyman nodded and walked behind the counter, put his satchel down, and lifted the casing of the old machine. He shook his head and looked up at Homer. "How long has it been this way?"

Homer's head jerked back and he peered under the peaked cap. The handyman had spoken with the shrill voice of a woman. Two glossy black eyes met his in a sharp, brown face that reminded him of a picture he'd seen of a mouse woman dressed in a long gown. He looked down: her name was embroidered over the pocket of her shirt, Vienna. He thought Vienna was a place.

She pulled a brush out of her satchel and began dusting the insides of the cash register. "This is quite dirty," she said, happily. "You must keep a machine clean, like your body."

Then she smiled as if she had made a wonderful discovery. "I can repair it," she said. Her mouth was painted so red that it seemed to separate from her face when she spoke and her speech was clipped and imperfect.

Homer felt a sudden, cold draft move through the shop and fumbled at the top button of his shirt. "You're not from Clintock," he said.

"No, I am Sri Lankan." She paused, watching him as he backed toward the mirror. "I have been in the United States three months," she said.

He stepped behind the mirror and sat down, groping for the tissue box. He mopped his face with a handful of tissue, catching bits of fluff in the stubble on his chin. He wanted her out of his shop, but it was too late, so he turned his back to the mirror.

A bell rang and Homer twisted around to see who had come in. Billy Blum stood at the counter, his arms hooped around his father's shirts, watching the handyman. Homer shuddered when the boy blew a bubble that grazed the ecru Van Husen that was on top. When the gum was sucked back into Billy's mouth, Homer relaxed.

The handyman peered through the mirror, searching for him. He flinched under her steady black eyes, blurred by the glass, but he felt she saw straight through the mirror. She turned away abruptly and spoke to the boy.

"He is in there," she said.

Billy nodded his head. "Is he hiding?"

Her head jerked up and Homer heard a laugh like hidden bells. "No, I do not think so. He is busy. I will take your shirts."

Billy nodded and the handyman gave him a claim check to fill out.

"I get the pink copy," Billy said, ripping it off. He was gone.

She lay the order form on top of the shirts and turned back to the cash register. She loaded another roll of tape, clicked the casing into place and punched in numbers with her spidery brown fingers. The tape marched up the side of the machine. She turned towards the curtain draped across the doorway to the back of the shop. "Mister?" she said.

Homer jumped up and backed into the racks of clothes.

"Mister?" She closed her tool box noisily, and he heard sharp footsteps coming towards him. "You pay me now?"

"Send me a bill," he shouted.

"No, you must pay me cash." She had moved the curtain aside and was in the room with him. "What are you doing in those clothes, Mister?"

Homer pushed to the back of the rack and walked around it. "I was looking for a lost order," he said and walked swiftly past the woman, his heart pounding. Her squeaky voice played on his most tender nerves. "How much?"

When she left, he went straight back and stood behind the clothes again. He liked the dark, liked the way the clothes absorbed sound. After his mother died, he continued doing all the cleaning on the premises, but the noise of the machines and the bright light required to operate them annoyed him. He got a free copy of *Cleaners and Launderers* in the mail and read that many small shops used central plants. Now the soiled clothes were picked up at four and delivered clean two days later at seven in the morning. There was a flurry of business from seven-thirty to eight-thirty — people making drops on their way to work — and another rush from four to six. In between, Homer was alone with the clean, bagged clothes, his catalogs, and his Moments. He was never lonely. He felt intimately acquainted with everyone in town who wore the kinds of clothes that required cleaning. They were the only people worth knowing, his mother had said. That was the advantage of owning a cleaners.

*

THE HANDYMAN returned at six. "I brought you extra ribbons," she said, thumping his shoulder with her brown finger.

"Oh," Homer said. He was sunk in thought, contemplating his new Moment, a Biblical piece, and hadn't heard her come in. He stood up so suddenly that he stumbled against the mirror. She had sneaked in, bypassing the bells, and touched him.

She held a box up. "I will show you how to change a ribbon."

Homer slid along the mirror, his back pressed to the cold glass, edging toward the corner so he could sink into the back of the store.

The handyman shook the box at him. "Where are you going?" she asked, her black eyes nailing him to the wall. "Don't you like machines?"

He shook his head. He was thinking about John the Baptist and couldn't focus on her words. He thought the eyes in a severed head would be open, calm, and steady.

The woman touched his sleeve at the elbow. "Many Americans do not repair what is broken," she laughed. "Before I came to this country, I thought everybody here knows everything, but now I see you make machines in the factories and then throw them away when they break." She crossed her painted lips with a long finger. "I stayed in a church for seventeen days. They gave me socks, sweaters, magazines, but nothing to do. I found many things broken there: doors, a window, one old typewriter and I repaired it all." She smiled again. "Reverend said to me, 'Vienna, you're a regular handyman,' so when I applied for work, I wrote regular handyman on all the forms."

Homer sighed deeply. His heart was racing and he felt faint.

"I am making money to send home. My mother is old." She patted her back pocket, then hit the dollar sign on the cash register and it clanged open.

"Yes," Homer whispered and sat down. He needed to put his head between his knees.

She looked at him sharply. "Come here. You are not rich. You must learn to fix this yourself."

He quickly pulled himself to his feet and stood behind her, just out of reach. He was afraid she would touch his shirt again. She snapped the old ribbon out, talking, pointing, forcing him to feel the click of the casing, the way the pieces went together. He did as she said, trying to follow her rapid explanations through his fog.

"Do you understand what I am showing you?"

Her voice scraped along his inner ear, insulting him. He was not a child. "Yes, of course I understand," he shouted. "Do you think I'm retarded?"

She slammed the casing on the cash register and hurried around the counter. Homer surged and swelled. He leaned with both fists on the counter towering over her, full-sized for a moment. She tapped a bell under the carpet so it rang repeatedly and laughed. "You are one crazy American," she said in her high voice. "I am trying to help you."

"I don't want you," Homer shouted. He felt he spoke with unusual clarity, his words sharply enunciated, carefully pronounced, but strong. He liked yelling at her.

"Your shop rings like a temple," she said. "It's not right. I'll take the bells out for you."

"No, go away."

"Today you pay me eight ninety-five for the ribbon plus house call — give me fifteen dollars," she said.

Her rodent eyes under the khaki cap pierced him and he hit the cash key on the register and counted out her money. Then he turned and stepped behind the mirror.

"I got work to do," he shouted at the clothes as he entered the familiar darkness.

Behind the mirror, he watched her leave, zigzagging between the bells under the carpet and opening the door so smoothly that it didn't ring. Damn foreigner, he thought. When she was gone, he rushed out, pulled the shades, locked the door, hung the closed sign, ringing all the bells as he dashed about. Then he sat in the back with the lights out and breathed the deep smell of wool and cleaning solution and plastic bags. He closed his eyes and rubbed his head but he couldn't get her eyes out of his brain. I must be crazy, he thought. There is something wrong with me.

He stood up and felt his way to the back of the store, where Grace Lily's fur coat hung in summer storage. He pulled off the plastic bag and sat with the coat around him and gave himself up to shaking, muffled sobs.

*

THE NEXT MORNING she slipped in behind Myrna Smythe. Myrna

threw the mail at Homer and dashed out. He gathered it up, holding the catalogs to his chest, and hurried to the back, as if he hadn't seen the handyman; but she followed him behind the mirror and grabbed his arm. "Help me with this letter."

He shuddered, shook her off and backtracked to the cash register, shrinking from the brown envelope she thrust in his face.

"I don't understand these government orders," she said.

He snatched the letter. "If I read it, will you leave?"

"Yes, I will go."

He turned his back to her. She reminded him of somebody. It would be easy to etch her sharp cheek bone in plaster. His fingers were swollen and tender, as if he were beginning a new sculpture, and he fumbled with the thin letter; he couldn't get it out of the envelope. Finally, he ripped it down the middle and spread the letter on the counter. It was a form letter from Immigration. Vienna Fernando, refugee, female, thirty-four, single, incomplete application for I-94.

"I must get this I-94. I have no identification without it."

He nodded without looking at her and closed his eyes. "Your picture is wrong," he said. "The government wants a full view of one ear."

The woman laughed.

Homer backed up and looked beyond her, out the window. An unfamiliar black car was parked in front of the store.

She pulled off her cap and pushed her hair back. "Which ear?" she said, giggling. The ear was sharp and small; a sculptor would scrape out the fullness under the cheekbone, to accent the lines of the skull.

"I don't know," he said. "I'm busy." He made a show of looking at his watch, then stepped behind the mirror and walked straight to his work bench where the new Moment in History was half-finished: the moment Salome lifted her veil to accept the head of John the Baptist. He had enjoyed forming that head. The nose was long and thin, the chin firm, with a cropped beard, the eyes clear, well-lit tunnels. Homer had thought John would have long, Jesus hair, but it writhed out of his head like snakes. The dreadlocks bothered him at first but he grew to like the effect. The piece would be finished when he found material for Salome's veils and could complete her face. When he pulled aside her veil, her features would be revealed and he could continue. He stared at the scene, trying to hear the music she would dance to, and he didn't move until the foreigner rang all the bells on her way out.

The next day, he saw her at the door through the mirror and froze with his hand suspended over Herodias, Salome's mother, sitting with her husband, the king. It was the mother who wanted the head. The handyman was looking for him through the mirror, and the taste of his breakfast eggs rose in his throat. Something was draped over her left arm — he couldn't make it out. She smiled at her reflection, adjusted her cap, and peered around the cash register.

"Mister?"

He was sure she could hear his heart banging against the wall of his chest. He didn't breathe.

She laid a garment on the counter, filled out a slip, then zigzagged out without ringing any of the bells.

The material shimmered as Homer approached it, red and gold, with a silver thread. He slipped his hands under the fabric, palms down, so his fingers wouldn't snag the cloth, and lifted it. The material diffused the sunlight like stained glass. He had never touched anything so beautiful. He held it to his cheek and closed his eyes. It was his mother's nightgown and the veil of Salome.

Her photograph lay on the counter with a note. "This is my sari, pure silk. How do you like the picture? The ear is okay?" She had pinned her hair against her scalp so her left ear was clearly visible and the hair curved around her chin on the right. She looked softer without her cap, less mouselike in the three-quarter view. The ridge along her cheek bone was full, as if she were suppressing her laugh. Her lips parted to expose one tooth, not a smile, and her eyes were opaque black dots on the shiny photograph. She had checked Monday on the order ticket. The sari must be ready Monday.

*

BUT SHE DIDN'T COME Monday, or Tuesday. Her silk hung with the fur coat, sleek and shining through the bag. Homer smoothed it frequently, to be sure it stayed flat. He thought of hanging it next to the cash register, so she could get it herself and he wouldn't have to come out, but he was afraid somebody might steal it or soil it.

Wednesday, after the morning rush, he was working again on

Herodias. He softened the bend in her nose with the scaler and tinted her cheeks with red spots, reflections from her dress. Her carmine velvet was ready, but the catalogs had nothing for Salome. Since he'd touched the sari, he knew that her gown must be tremulous with its own light.

He heard movement in the front of the shop and looked up. The handyman was silently stalking him, setting her feet on the solid places in the carpet. He held his breath and looked at the sari. He should get it for her.

"The bell on the door is ugly," she shouted when she reached the counter. "I will fix you a new one that will ring beautiful when people come in."

He set the mother Herodias on her throne, her left elbow on the arm of the chair, her head jutting towards Herod like a feeding crane, and stood up.

"Also, we will take them out of the floor."

Homer watched her through the mirror. He wanted to talk about the sari, but when she started around the counter, he hurried to stop her from coming back, tripping over a stool and kicking it into the doorway. "Now look here," he said, panting.

She picked up the stool and set it between them. "I will help you and you help me. It's the American way," she said. "Is my picture okay?"

He nodded and stared at her cap. "What do you want?"

She waved an envelope. "What is this for?"

It was addressed to Occupant.

"Junk mail," Homer said. "Leave me alone." He rapped the cash register with his knuckles. "This works fine. Why do you come back?"

"I like you," she said.

Homer pressed his hands to his face and closed his eyes.

"You are tall, a nice man." She shook the envelope. "I don't know other American people. I always find you here."

It occurred to him that she might think they were friends. "I'm not your friend," he said, straightening up suddenly. "I'm busy." He stepped behind the mirror and turned the clothes sorter on so the swinging hangars of bagged clothes rolled past him in alphabetical order.

Through the mirror, he watched her tear open the letter. She held it just in front of her pointed nose and moved her hand as she read. She needs glasses, he thought. Then she ripped it into four pieces, threw it at the cash register and left, ringing all the bells. He could see her through the plate glass window, standing on the sidewalk, with her back to his shop, staring across the square. She pulled off her cap and pushed her hair behind her ears with jerks of her hands. Clyde Walnut stopped beside her, to check a parking meter. Vienna turned in his direction and nodded but Walnut didn't take notice. Homer watched her for several minutes, then switched off the clothes sorter and sat down behind the mirror.

A single bell rang and he looked up. It was Vienna. She threw her cap on the counter, pulled the stool over to the front door, stood on it, and strained toward the cow bell at the top. From the back she looked like a child in a play suit, with green high-top basketball shoes and a hammer swinging from her belt.

Homer stood up slowly, walked around the mirror and towards the door, setting off all the bells. He felt drugged. "Get down," he said. "I'll get it." She jumped off the chair and stood with her back to him. He stretched his arms over his head, straining unused muscles, and moaned as he lifted the bell from the door frame and handed it to her.

"Thank you," she said. "Here." She slapped the installation instructions for the electric eye in his hand.

He opened the paper, turning it until he found the top. STOP. READ ALL INSTRUCTIONS BEFORE PROCEEDING. Exactly, he thought. One must never go forward until ready. Read everything first. He glanced at the handyman. She had lined up all the parts and was staring at them intently. After a minute she reversed the order of two wires and studied the arrangement again.

"You didn't read this," he said, waving the instruction sheet.

"If you look at something carefully," she said, "and see every part, you can know how it works and fit it together." Her hair fell across her face and she shoved it back. A gray hair sprouted at her part. "Americans don't look slowly. You are too fast. That is your problem."

I do, Homer thought. I am not fast. He saw everything in single frames, not moving or run together. He saw so slowly that he missed the connections.

She began the installation, with her back to him, talking. "When

I come here, everybody tell me, I am lucky to be in America. You don't say that." She drilled three holes. "Do you believe in luck?"

He started to nod, then shook his head.

"I don't like luck. It doesn't work." She handed him an orange cord with a three-prong plug. "Do we need an adapter?"

He stared at the plug, twisting the hard cord in his fingers. "Yes. Yes." He thrust the cord back in her hand, but she missed it. He didn't wait, but hurried to the back, through the hanging clothes, pulled out the shoe box labeled electricity and found three adapters. He scooped them all up and ran back, panting. He opened his hand, offering her the adapters as if they were chocolates.

She chose the beige one.

He plugged in the cord and she passed her hand through the electric eye. Nothing.

"Okay," she said. "Don't worry. I can fix it."

He pulled the plug and sat down. He liked the way she talked without looking right at him. He closed his eyes to listen.

"Okay," she said again. "Everybody says to me 'You okay, Vienna?' At first I was slow to answer. I wanted to explain about my mother but they smiled and said 'okay, see you' and were gone. So now I smile also and answer 'everything okay.' "

"Is your mother . . ." Homer couldn't find the word. He opened his eyes. "Is she . . ."

"Okay?"

He nodded.

"No, she is not." The handyman's thin voice rose abruptly. She stopped working momentarily, but didn't turn around. "She is alone in my country."

"My mother is dead," Homer said.

Myrna Smythe struck Vienna with the door when she burst in with the mail, fluttering her cow eyes in Homer's direction. "Oh, excuse me," she said. "Am I interrupting something, Homer?"

Homer stared at her, startled, and Vienna stepped back to let her pass. Myrna slapped the mail in Homer's hand and touched her hot, minty mouth to his ear. "Homer," she whispered, "ain't you afraid of that foreigner?" Then she backed out of the store, winking and smirking. He thought of running after her, out into the street, snatching the mailbag and dumping it over her head.

"Mister?" Vienna put the cord in his hand. When he plugged it in, she wiggled her fingers through the light and a bell rang. "It works," she said, smiling and laughing at the same time. "Very modern."

He took a deep breath and looked away, then crumpled the instruction sheet and slipped behind the mirror, exhausted, to sit on his chair and watch her pack up the tools.

"Good bye, Mister," she called when she finished.

"Thank you," he said, but she was gone. The sari still hung in the back and he had said nothing.

The bell rang again and he looked up. "Mister, you owe me forty-three dollars for materials. The installation is free."

Homer groaned. "Take it out of the cash register," he called. "I'm busy." He walked to the back wall and leaned into the fur coat, ashamed.

*

HE SAW HER hurry past his plate glass window later, head down against a strong wind, hand on her satchel, cap pulled low over her eyes. Her beige jumpsuit was crisp and pressed and she still looked like a professional, but he saw now that she was unmistakably a woman, slight and delicate. He wondered how he had been fooled the first day. Expectations, he thought, we get what we expect and I expected a man.

For the rest of the day, his stomach cramped every time the bells in the floor rang. When he looked up and saw it wasn't her, he went limp. He had no strength to wait on customers. The bells would have to come out, he thought. She laughs like those bells. He pulled back the carpet and stared at the maze of wires that connected them. He kicked at a wire and the whole network pealed. He wondered if he could just yank it out like he pulled kudzu off his mother's trees years ago. No. He dropped the carpet and walked around the counter to look up the installer's number.

She came in as he was staring at the directory, holding out a piece of paper torn from a legal pad. He backed away.

"I need help with my English, spelling."

He shook his head.

"You are American; you can correct my letter."

He watched her reflection in the mirror without turning around.

At the edge of the glass, he glimpsed a middle-aged man with deep circles under his eyes, wispy hair, a mole on his chin, like his mother had, and a limp, oxford-cloth shirt threadbare at the collar and as washed out as the man's skin. Homer jerked his face toward the image to see the man better, then covered his eyes. That's me, he thought. That's me.

Vienna slapped her paper on the counter, opened her satchel, and pulled out wire clippers. She tapped her toe on the carpet, ringing the bells. "I hate that," she said.

He read her letter. The handwriting was copy-book perfect, round and generous, and the composition of her letter was nearly perfect. He took it in the back to make some changes, but his cramped printing looked childish next to her full vowels and bold capitals.

When he was finished, he brought the letter to her. "Your cleaning is ready."

She carefully folded the letter and stuck it in her pocket. She was pulling electrical tape off the floor and winding it into a black, sticky ball. Homer felt a curious desire to touch her, to comfort her the way you would reassure a child who lost her mother, just touch her shoulder. She seemed to get smaller each time he saw her.

Doc Proffet came in coughing and wiping his eyes. He stumbled over the rolled-up carpet and caught the counter to keep himself from falling. Frowning at Vienna, he turned his head sideways to examine Homer. "Your mama'd roll over in her grave, Homer," he said. "Stick with your own kind."

Then three more customers trooped in, in quick succession, walking around the brown woman tugging at wires on the floor, commenting on the weather, asking him if he were remodeling.

"I didn't think you dealt with foreigners," Clyde Walnut said, writing a check.

Homer blushed and looked at Vienna. She was standing in the corner, rolling the wires around her arm, hand to elbow. He took Clyde's check and stared into the cash register until he left. The handyman concentrated on her work so intently, it was possible she hadn't heard.

"You don't need these wires," she said. "Perhaps I can use them somewhere else."

"Fine," he rasped.

"These people talk slyly, always joking," Vienna said. "They think foreigners are stupid." She laughed, tied off the coil of wire, and slid her arm through the center, then held her hand out, as if to touch him.

Homer instinctively drew back.

Her hand closed into a fist and she struck the counter as she spoke. "They look at you, Mister, like they look at me, with snake in their mouths."

He shook his head and covered the side of his face with his big hand. "I'm busy," he said and went to the back. He heard nothing for a minute, then the bell rang. He should have paid her. He didn't think of it in time. He should have told Walnut to shut up. He leaned against the fur coat, staring at the sari, waiting for her to come back and demand money, but she didn't. He sank back into the coat and closed his eyes, taking in shallow, convulsive breaths, trying to stop the movement within him. His internal organs were shifting places; his lungs collapsed into the small intestine as he struggled to breathe. His inner ears buzzed, his throat was dry. He held on to the sleeves of the coat with both hands, but was falling again, was burning, and his ears drummed with sound. It wasn't dark enough. He closed his eyes, but couldn't get it dark enough. Finally he turned his face to the satin lining of the coat and let his tears streak the smooth soft skin.

He saw her in the sari with bells hung around her head and on the hem of the silk, tinkling as she walked and she held out her hands to him and, as he felt his arms rise, his mother pushed them down and stood in front of him so he couldn't see the woman in silk and he tried to lift his arms again, but they weren't there and he tried to walk around his mother but he had no legs and his eyes grew bigger and deeper so his mother became hazy, transparent, like his two-way mirror, and the woman was standing there, the silk sari undone, but covering her hair and face and body and he tried again to lift it off.

The bell rang twice. He stood up suddenly, disoriented, his blood racing through his body, heating up his skin. It was Myrna Smythe. He pushed his hair back, licked his lips, and stepped to the doorway.

"Homer, you look burned," she said. "Have you been lying out in the sun, working on your tan?" She closed one of her cow eyes, then opened it, and stared at him, smiling, waiting for an answer.

His mouth was too dry to speak. Myrna knew better, he thought. He never went outside; it was laughable. He grabbed his chest and began to laugh. It rolled up and out of him, rippling from his throat, then from his stomach, from the soles of both feet. His uncontrollable belly laugh took over his body and made his head ache. He blushed and wiped his eyes, grabbing for the tissues. He couldn't stop laughing.

"That sure is a good one," he gasped over and over. "That's rich."

"Something's happened to you, Homer," Myrna said. She backed out of the store, staring at him bent over the counter, holding on with one hand, banging his fist on the formica.

*

SHE returned at three, with the letter. He was braiding Salome's hair, but when he saw the beige cap, he covered the Moment and hurried to the front counter. He tried to smile.

"I fixed the letter," she said. "What do you think?"

He took it and leaned against the mirror. "Good," he said.

"This window is dirty, Mister. I'll clean while you read my letter." Her head bobbed as she talked.

"No, it's all right."

"I'll get some water," she said and stepped around the counter and through the curtain to the back.

"Stop," he said. "You can't go back there." But she didn't hear him. Maybe she didn't understand. He stood with her letter in his hand, written on yellow paper. His duty to the letter paralyzed him momentarily, then he put it on the counter with his pencil on top and went after her. He never let anybody go in the back of his store.

She was in his room. "Where is the light?" she asked.

"No light," he said. "Go back to the front." Bending over her, he felt bloated and huge. She smelled faintly of lemons.

She turned her flashlight to his face. "Oh," she gasped. "What's that?" The Moments in History swayed slowly from the ceiling. Her light moved from scene to scene, flashing on one, then going on to the next. "They are beautiful," she said. "I must see." She put her hand on his wrist. "Show me."

He trembled and grabbed her hand to keep from shaking it off his arm. He started to laugh and she turned toward him. "Mister?" she said.

"Could you call me Homer?" He pulled her to him, crossing his arms around her narrow back. The bill of her hat hit his shoulder and fell to the floor. She dropped the flashlight. He patted her thick hair. "You poor little thing," he said.

She moved in his arms and he held her tighter. He wanted to kiss her smooth head, but didn't dare. The idea sent a wave of heat over him and he pressed her closer. Her head rocked against his chest and she struggled to get free of him. He realized he was holding her too tightly but couldn't relax his muscles. "I'm so sorry," he said. "So sorry."

"Homer." Her voice was muffled but the sound of his name released the tension from his arms and he was able to relax his grip. He let go of her abruptly and they staggered backwards, away from each other. He covered his face to muffle his gasping breaths. She touched his elbow but he shook his head and turned away.

When she found the switch, the fluorescent light over the work bench fluttered on. "I know . . ." her squeaky voice faltered. "When you are alone all the time, sometime . . ."

He dropped his hands and carefully turned around. She stood there, hatless, her hair wild around her small face, a slight figure in the dim room. Her eyes were brown, not black, and as she looked at him, she blushed and he raised his fingers to his own hot cheek.

She threw one hand up in the air and let it drop at her side. "I can't say it in English."

"Look," he said, and swept back the sheet that covered Salome and John the Baptist.

She picked up her flashlight and let the beam float over each of the figures. Herod reclined on his throne, smiling, red cheeked, his thick hands clasped over his belly; and the beautiful Herodias, his brother's wife, leaned with her red lips on his ear lobe, her hand under his velvet robe. The naked, faceless Salome stood on an elevated stage before the royal pair, one arm crossed in front of her face, the other stretched towards her mother. Vienna brushed her light over the figure, then touched the rotating platform with her hand. Salome spun around, her arm outstretched, her blank face blocked. At the edge of the platform the executioner stood, dressed in black, legs spread, elbows bent under the weight of the silver platter bearing the head of the prophet. Vienna turned her light on the head.

"Look at his eyes," she said. "They are ice like yours, but with the hair of Shiva."

Homer sat down heavily in his chair.

"Why has the girl no eyes and no clothes?" Vienna turned off her light and touched Salome's featureless face with her finger. "Is she blind?"

"No," said Homer slowly, shaking his head. "I can't see her eyes yet. I must clothe her, veil her face to know how she looks."

Vienna nodded. "Yes, she will be beautiful." She slipped her flashlight into the loop on her uniform. "I will make her a sari, and . . ." She paused, spreading her fingers across her face. "What do you call it?"

"Veil."

"I will make her a veil, then you will see her face, yes?" She put her left hand on his shoulder and stuck out her right for him to shake. "We can be . . . partners."

He swiveled his chair towards her and noticed that her central incisors were crooked when she smiled. She looked young in the dim light. He stroked his chapped lips with his fingertips and stared longingly at the fur coat for a moment, then closed his eyes and firmly clasped her hand.

Photo: Charles Coskran

KATHLEEN COSKRAN was born in California but lived in Georgia until she graduated from Agnes Scott College in Decatur. She joined the Peace Corps and met her future husband, also a Volunteer, while teaching in Ethiopia. After two years in Washington, D.C., they returned to East Africa where their first son was born in Nyeri, Kenya, in 1970. Coskran, her husband, and their five children now live in Minneapolis. She was a Montessori teacher and Director of the Children's Research Center at Lake Country School in Minneapolis from 1979-86. She is currently a graduate student at the University of Minnesota, working on an M.A. in English with an Emphasis on Writing. She was a Loft/ Mentor winner in 1986 and is a Regional Writers Series winner for 1988.